Building Node.js REST API
with
TDD Approach

Parri Pandian

10 Steps Complete Guide for
Node.js, Express.js & MongoDB RESTful Service
with
Test-Driven Development

I dedicate this book to my wife and kids.

Table of Contents

PART THREE: Developing & Testing the REST API

PART ONE: Concepts for Building the REST API

Chapter 1: *Introduction*

1.1. Introduction

IN THIS BOOK, we will build a Node.js RESTful service from the scratch with Test-Driven Development (TDD) approach. To begin with, we will go through the list of frameworks and tools that we will be using for all the phases: from the design, development, and testing to familiarize ourselves before diving into each the action.

We will learn the central concepts of RESTful Service and TDD that we need know to build a REST API at the start of this book itself. Wouldn't be fun to learn the nitty-gritty of those central concepts while going through the whole process in each step? So, we will continue to learn all the necessary details of the big-picture concepts as we travel along each chapter and section as required to make it learning by doing the process.

We will go through all the crucial steps of building any software system one by one in the natural flow so that we can absorb the concept in each of the steps effectively and create the system efficiently.

Below are the crucial steps that we are going to walk through in this book while building the REST API with TDD approach.

- **Requirement** of the system,
- **Conceptualize** the system behavior to satisfy the requirements,
- **Architect** the big picture of the system that we are going to build,

- **Design** the system with the appropriate level of depth so that we know affront what path we are going to walk through,
- **Develop** the system with prescribed technology and approach.
- **Test** the built system to conform to the requirements that started the whole process of creating it.

I can assure that your journey through this book will be an enjoyable learning experience. Let's build it.

1.2. Frameworks & Tools

IN THIS CHAPTER, we will go through the frameworks and the tools that we will be using in this book to build a RESTful API from scratch.

1.2.1. Development Frameworks

This section contains a list of frameworks that we will use to develop the RESTful service.

Node

First in this list is NodeJS, apparently as this book is about building a NodeJS API. Node.js is a javascript runtime built on Chrome's V8 JavaScript engine which is Google's open source high-performance JavaScript engine, written in C++ and used in Google Chrome. Since the V8 runs on the multiple platforms such as Windows, macOS, and Linux, Node.js runtime is also running on those platforms as well.

As an asynchronous event-driven JavaScript runtime, Node is designed to build scalable network applications. Check the Node's website https://nodejs.org for more details and documentation.

Express

Express (https://expressjs.com/) is a minimal and flexible Node.js web application framework that provides a robust set of features for web and mobile applications. With a myriad of HTTP utility methods and middleware at your disposal, creating a robust API is quick and easy.

Express provides a thin layer of fundamental web application features, without obscuring Node.js features that you know and love. Many popular frameworks are based on Express which can be found in this link https://expressjs.com/en/resources/frameworks.html.

MongoDB

MongoDB (https://www.mongodb.com) is a document database with the scalability and flexibility that you want with the querying and indexing that you need.

MongoDB stores data in flexible, JSON-like documents, meaning fields can vary from document to document and data structure can be changed over time. The document model maps to the objects in your application code, making data easy to work with.

Mongoose

Mongoose (http://mongoosejs.com/) is an elegant MongoDB object modeling for node.js.

Mongoose provides a straight-forward, schema-based solution to model your application data. It includes built-in typecasting, validation, query building, business logic hooks and more, out of the box.

1.2.2. Testing Frameworks

This section contains a list of frameworks that we will use to test the

RESTful service with Test-Driven Development approach in this book.

Mocha

As per its website, Mocha is a feature-rich JavaScript test framework running on Node.js and in the browser, making asynchronous testing simple and fun. Mocha tests run serially, allowing for flexible and accurate reporting while mapping uncaught exceptions to the correct test cases.

We will be using this framework to run the unit tests and integration tests for the RESTful service that we are going to create in this book. You can check out the website https://mochajs.org/ to know more about it and also documentation for its usage.

Chai

Chai is a TDD / BDD assertion library for node and browser which can be used with any javascript testing framework. Chai has several interfaces that we can choose from BDD (Behavior-Driven Development) and TDD (Test-Driven Development) styles.

BDD style, which is chain-capable, provides expressive language and readable form. TDD style offers the traditional feel of assertion for testing. Refer http://chaijs.com/ for more information about this library.

Sinon

Sinon library is used to create standalone spies, stubs and mocks for JavaScript. As it works with any unit testing framework, we will use with Mocha for the RESTful service codebase testing along with chai assertion library. Check out the http://sinonjs.org/ for Sinon related details.

1.2.3. Development Tools

This section contains a list of tools that we will use to develop and test the RESTful service.

IDE (Integrated Development Environment)

To build an API with any language or framework, we need to have a development environment set up at the local machine, the developer's desktop/laptop.

You can use any of the operating systems (Windows/macOS/Linux) available out there as per your choice and convenience. Depends on the OS of your choice, there are many IDEs available in these options, free/paid. Each developer has his/her own choice of the IDE as well. Whatever your choice may be, for building the REST API described in this book you would need a NodeJS development supported IDE.

Below are the few of the famous IDEs that you can choose from depends on your OS and you are comfortable with.

1. WebStorm (https://www.jetbrains.com/webstorm/)
2. IntelliJ IDEA (https://www.jetbrains.com/idea)
3. Visual Studio Code (https://code.visualstudio.com/)
4. Sublime Text (https://www.sublimetext.com/)
5. Atom (https://atom.io/)

Chapter 2: *RESTful Service*

2.1. RESTful Service

IN THIS CHAPTER, we will look at what is a RESTful service and the characteristics that define it. Also, we will go over the HTTP methods that can be used to expose the functionalities of the RESTful service through APIs.

2.2. What Is A RESTful Service?

REST IS AN acronym for **Re**presentational **S**tate **T**ransfer which is coined by Roy Fielding in 2000 in his dissertation Architectural Styles and the Design of Network-based Software Architectures (https://www.ics.uci.edu/~fielding/pubs/dissertation/top.htm). REST is an architectural style which defined certain constraints for building a distributed system using the HTTP protocol.

RESTful service is any distributed system written in any language and exposes its functionalities over the HTTP protocol within the REST architectural style constraints. It's a client-server architecture web service which presents resources through certain representations along with self-descriptive messages.

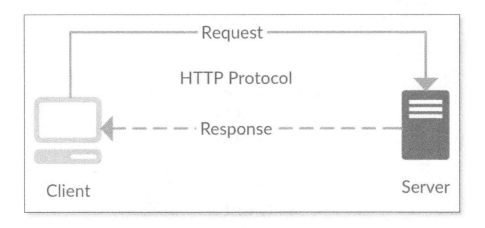

2.3. Characteristics of RESTful Service

ROY FIELDING ADDED specific constraints to the REST architecture to call any distributed system as RESTful service. We will discuss all those main constraints which make up the characteristics of the RESTful service in the below section.

2.3.1. Constraint 1: Client-Server

With the traditional web application, where the server renders the view components with the required data for each of the requests, this first and fore-most REST principle tries to de-couple the user interface concerns from the data storage concerns with the client-server architecture style.

This separation of concerns principle makes the distributed system's server components scalable by removing any view rendering related concerns while improving the user interface portable across multiple platforms. Thus, the same server components can be used by multiple clients on different platforms with various view specific implementation with the same response from the server.

2.3.2. Constraint 2: Stateless

This second constraint forces the server not to store any session related information for any request. It's the client's responsibility to store and manage any session related information at the client side and send all the information related to request to the server so that server doesn't need to use any of the previous request details or any stored session details at the server side to serve the current request.

This constraint provides the RESTful service with the visibility, reliability, and scalability. We will see how these properties are available to the server components in the client-server architecture with REST principles applied.

1. **Visibility**: Since each request contains all the information need to process it and respond with the required information, the server does not need to look beyond the single request to understand it's nature. Thus, the visibility of the server is improving.

2. **Reliability**: If any particular request is failed at the server side, the server side components will not be impacted as any other further requests do not depend on the previous requests. Thus, the reliability of the RESTful service is improved because then it can still serve the requests even after any partial failures previously.

3. **Scalability**: It is improved because the server component doesn't need to store any information between the requests, it can quickly free-up the resources once any request is processed and responded. Also, this characteristics simplifies the RESTful service's implementation as it does not have to manage any resource usage across requests.

Having a trade-off just like any architectural choices is inevitable even though stateless constraint provides several benefits to the RESTful service, Since the server does not maintain shared context across the requests, the network performance is reduced for repetitive data sent in for a series of requests.

2.3.3. Constraint 3: Cache

To improve the reduced network performance introduced by the previous constraint, a new constraint Cache is added to the REST architecture. With this constraint, the server component can label the data in the response for a request as cacheable or non-cacheable. When the client receives the cacheable response, it can re-use this response for the same request later.

This ability to cache the response at the client side improves the network efficiency, scalability, and user-perceived performance by reducing the number calls to fetch the response for the same request repeatedly.

2.3.4. Constraint 4: Uniform Interface

The main feature that distinguishes the REST architecture from other web architectures is the Uniform Interface constraint. This constraint enforces the component's behavior or interfaces to be uniform across all the components even though the implementation varies.

REST has been defined with below four interface related constraints to provide the uniform interface across its components.

1. **Resource**: It's the critical abstraction of information in REST. A resource can be any information that can be named: a document, image or temporal service, a collection of other resources a non-virtual object and so on. Also, a resource is a conceptual mapping to a set of entities. A resource must be identified by a resource identifier, URL or URN.

2. **Representation**: The resources are manipulated by the REST

components using the representation to capture the current or modified state of the resource. The representation consists of data and metadata about the data. The data format of representation is known as a media type.

3. **Self-Descriptive Message:** The response from the server should contain the media type for the resource's representation to the client. So that the client knows how to parse and process the data it received for any request.

4. **HATEOAS:** It's the acronym for Hypermedia As The Engine Of Application State. It means that once the client receives the response from the server, the response should have links for other application states so that the client can use those links to move to the next state of the application.

2.4. RESTful Service Operations

WE USE RESTFUL service to perform below four principal operations on the resources that it exposes. These are called CRUD operations.

1. **Create**: With this operation, a new resource is created.
2. **Read**: To retrieve the representation of the resource we use the read operation of the RESTful service.
3. **Update**: Once the resource is created, we can modify the resource details with the update operation.
4. **Delete**: If an existing resource to be removed from the RESTful system, the delete operation is used.

2.5. HTTP Methods

SINCE THE RESTFUL service is built upon HTTP protocol for external communication, in this section, we will see how the API endpoints are accessed via the HTTP verbs/methods for different functionalities. Also, how the RESTful service's CRUD operations are initiated with the appropriate HTTP methods.

2.5.1. POST Method

The create operation is performed when a request is sent with the POST HTTP method. New resource's representation should be sent as request body to create it in the REST system.

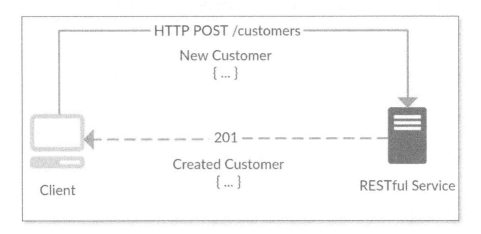

Example:

```
curl --request POST \
  --url http://localhost:3000/customers \
  --header 'Content-Type: application/json' \
  --data '{
  "firstName": "John",
  "lastName": "Smith",
  "email": "john.smith@example.com",
  "phoneNumber": "9876543210",
  "address": "100 E Street",
  "city": "New York",
  "state": "NY",
  "zipCode": "10000",
  "country": "USA"
}'
```

2.5.2. GET Method

To fetch the existing resource's representation, the request needs to be sent with the GET HTTP method. The response would be containing the resource's representation with additional metadata along with media type of the response.

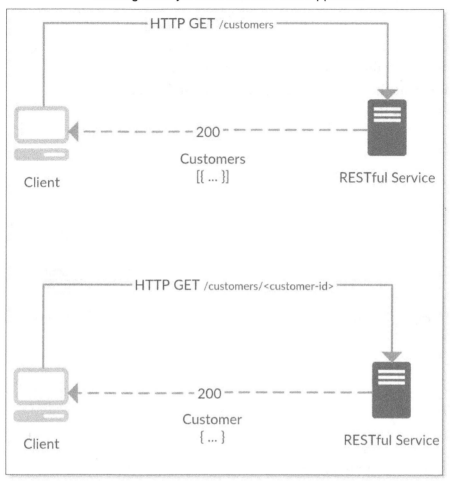

Examples:

```
curl --request GET \
  --url http://localhost:3000/customers

curl --request GET \
  --url http://localhost:3000/customers/
5b19e5f017d1aa0e55ed8d96
```

2.5.3. PUT Method

To modify the existing resource, we can send a request with PUT HTTP method along with the new representation of the existing resource as the request body.

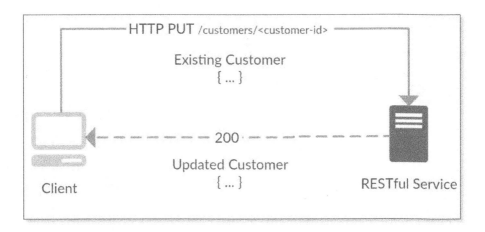

Example:

```
curl --request PUT \
  --url http://localhost:3000/customers/
5b19e5f017d1aa0e55ed8d96 \
  --header 'Content-Type: application/json' \
  --data '{
    "_id": "5b19e5f017d1aa0e55ed8d96",
    "firstName": "John",
    "lastName": "Smith",
    "email": "john.smith@example.com",
    "phoneNumber": 1234567890,
    "address": "401 W Street",
    "city": "New York",
    "state": "NY",
```

```
    "zipCode": "10000",
    "country": "USA",
    "__v": 0
}'
```

2.5.4. DELETE Method

To perform delete operation on the existing resource, we have to use the DELETE HTTP method while sending the request to the RESTful service with the URL of the resource which needs to be removed from the system.

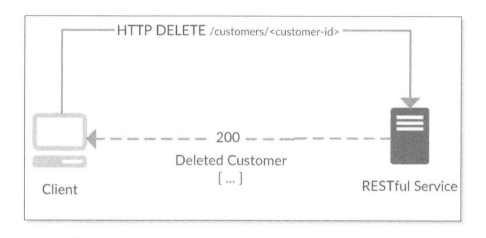

Example:

```
curl --request DELETE \
  --url http://localhost:3000/customers/
5b19e5f017d1aa0e55ed8d96
```

Chapter 3: *Test Driven Development*

3.1. Test Driven Development

TRADITIONALLY, MOST OF the legacy systems had been developed first and tested later for the expected behavior as per the requirements. This approach left many execution paths are untested and prone to bugs be hidden within the systems. Many of these bugs have been found during the testing phase, and some are in the production with unexpected crashes or issues. Increased technical debt like this left those applications with less maintainability and increased the cost of maintenance and confusing and complicated to add any new features to enhance the system.

Nowadays, with the expectation of continuous delivery with high quality forces developers to embed the automated testing within their development phase. This testing ensures that more bugs are captured while the functionality is being developed so that they could be fixed along with the feature.

With the popularity and broad adaptation of agile development methodology and pair programming, tests are being written before the actual functionality being developed to ensure that the system will be tested against the expected specification for the business requirement. More tests are supposed to be prepared to make sure the systems' conformity to design specification and a robust system's delivery to the end users.

The approach of writing the tests first and then the confirming or passing functionality code is called Test Driven Development (TDD). This book's primary goal is to discuss the Test Driven Development approach and how it can be applied to develop an API in NodeJS with ExpressJS and MongoDB.

In this chapter, we will go through what is TDD, its benefits and how it is integrated with the development process.

3.2. What Is TDD?

LET'S SEE WHAT the Test-Driven Development (TDD) method is. It's a development approach where the developer writes the small test for functionality and then writing the code for that feature to pass the previously written test and then refactor the code without changing the behavior. Then repeat the steps with more enhanced tests until both the tests and codes are satisfying the functional specification of a requirement.

The small test that was written is called Unit Test. To test a small unit of code, we usually write a unit test. Without any dependency, the single unit of code can be tested with the help of unit test. In the TDD approach, we need to write the unit test for the functionality before the actual code.

3.2.1. TDD Steps

Here are steps that we need to follow while employing the TDD approach.

- **Step 1**: Write a partial unit test.
- **Step 2**: Run the unit test to fail it (As we haven't written the actual code yet).
- **Step 3**: Write the minimal code for the functionality to the pass the partial unit test.

- **Step 4**: Run the unit test,
  - **Step 4a**: If it passes, refactor the code without changing the behavior and without failing the test again.
  - **Step 4b**: If it fails, go back to the Step 3 to write/ modify the code minimally to pass the unit test.
- **Step 5**: Repeat the Step 1 with the more enhanced unit test for that functionality.

3.2.2. TDD Process Flow

Here is the process flow diagram of the Test Driven Development approach.

Building Node.js REST API with TDD Approach

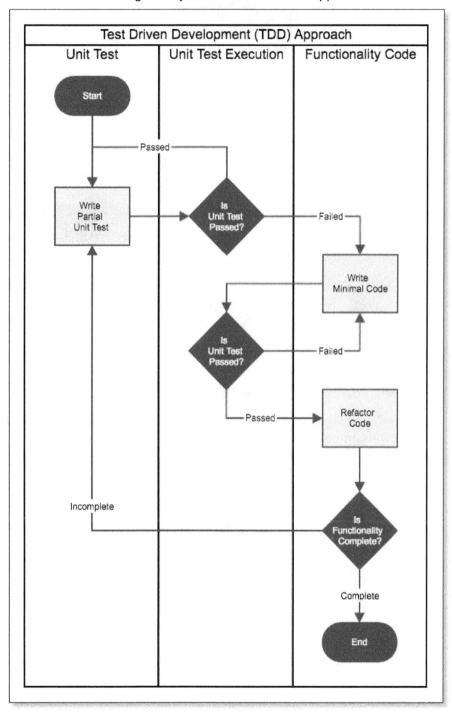

3.3. Why Is TDD Needed

WRITING THE TESTS during the development phase would be time-consuming, and the developer needs to have the required skill set to do so, what are the benefits we could get out of TDD?

3.3.1. Benefits of TDD

There are many benefits of using TDD in the day-to-day development process. Below are few of those.

1. The quality code will be developed which conforms to the requirements specifications.
2. Development time to be faster with the TDD approach over the time.
3. Maintainability of the code base will be easy as there will be tests for the existing code base. This approach will make sure that new changes affecting the current features will be captured at the earliest. This way those failing code will be fixed along with the new changes.
4. The unit tests used in test-driven development will be acting as the regression test suites for the whole codebase. So that any breaking changes will be captured during the development phase.
5. All the unit tests will be acting as live executable documenta-

tion of the code base that we maintain as these test cases will always be running in every development cycle to make sure that all the components are working as designed.

6.   Regularly, the existing code base might be cleaned up with the refactoring happening at any new feature additions are enhancements, this will ensure that the technical debt will be reduced and the code will be cleaner over the time.

7.   Debugging time will be reduced as the unit test it isolated and tests the small portion of the codebase, it will be quicker to debug to find the bug and fix it.

3.3.2. Drawbacks of TDD

As there are many benefits we can get out of TDD approach, there are few drawbacks as well.

1.   The organization needs to take into account the initial ramp-up time is necessary for the developers to do TDD as it has a learning curve to adapt to daily development activities.

2.   As a developer, they need to take a different approach from the traditional development approach as the TDD will force them to think of better software design and this will require time and effort to adapt.

PART TWO: *Design & Setup for Building the REST API*

Chapter 4: *Customer Information System*

4.1. Requirements

TO DEMONSTRATE THE NodeJS API development, we will create a system for storing and retrieving customer information. We can call it **Customer Information System**. Eventually, we will use NodeJS, ExpressJS, and MongoDB to create it as a RESTful service, which we can name it as **Customer Service**.

The system will have specific functionalities to manage customer information. These functionalities of the system can be exposed through API, which will be built into the system itself.

4.1.1. Functionalities

In our system, the first thing we have to do is functionality to add a new customer. Then we can update an existing customer detail. Once we have created the customer and eventually we want to read the customer detail, we can also get a list of customers from our system.

Below are the different functionalities or operations or end-points that we can create in our Customer Service RESTful API.

1. Add Customer API

In this API endpoint, we have to send a new customer detail in the request and the service will create the customer in the system. Once the customer creation is complete, the API will respond with the newly created customer detail. Here is the requirement specification for this API.

Add Customer	
HTTP Method	POST
API Endpoint	/customers
Request Path Parameter	None
Request Query Parameter	None
Request Body	Customer Details
Response Body	Created Customer Details
Response Status	200

2. Get Customer List API

With this API endpoint, we will be able to get a list of customers. This API endpoint will also have searching, filtering, and paging features. So that can search for customers with particular search criteria, apply some filtering conditions, and we can even get the result with pagination. Requirement specification for this functionality is as below.

Get Customers List	
HTTP Method	GET
API Endpoint	/customers
Request Path Parameter	None

Request Query Parameter	None
Request Body	None
Response Body	Fetched Customers List
Response Status	200

3. Get Customer API

Once the customer has been created or modified, we can get the detail for a particular customer via this API endpoint. Requirement specification for this functionality is as below.

Get Customer	
HTTP Method	GET
API Endpoint	/customers/:customerId
Request Path Parameter	customerId
Request Query Parameter	None
Request Body	None
Response Body	Fetched Customer Details
Response Status	200

4. Modify Customer API

In this operation, we will send the modified customer detail in the request to be persisted in the storage. Like the add customer API, this will also respond the modified customer detail in the response once it's completed the request. Requirement specification for this functionality is as below.

Modify Customer	
HTTP Method	PUT
API Endpoint	/customers/:customerId
Request Path Parameter	customerId
Request Query Parameter	None
Request Body	Customer Details
Response Body	Modified Customer Details
Response Status	200

5. Remove Customer API

We can also delete a customer from our system using this API endpoint. Once the customer has been removed from the system, this will respond with the customer detail back to the requested system. Requirement specification for this functionality is as below.

Remove Customer	
HTTP Method	DELETE
API Endpoint	/customers/:customerId
Request Path Parameter	customerId
Request Query Parameter	None
Request Body	None

Response Body	Removed Customer Details
Response Status	200

4.1.2. Customer Details

Since our system's primary purpose is to collect, store and retrieve the customer information, we need to define all fields or attributes of the customer information. The below table shows the attributes that we want to store in the storage for a customer.

Also, field type required flag and any constraints of each attribute. This additional information is essential so that the system can be designed, developed, and tested robustly.

Field Name	Field Type	Required?	Constraints
First Name	Text	Required	Minimum 2 Characters
Last Name	Text	Required	Minimum 1 Character
Email	Text	Required	Valid Email
Phone Number	Number	Required	Valid Phone Number
Address	Text	Not Required	
City	Text	Not Required	
State	Text	Not Required	
Zip Code	Number	Not Required	
Country	Text	Not Required	

4.2. Architecture / High Level Design

NOW THAT WE have the requirements for API we can go ahead with defining the architecture of the customer information system. This step is one of the essential steps before we begin the API development. Without clearly defining the architecture of the system we cannot build it without any issue.

Below image represents the system that we are building. Our system consists of a RESTful service and a database. The RESTful service, Customer Service, will be developed in NodeJS with Express JS. MongoDB will be used as a database for the service to interact with.

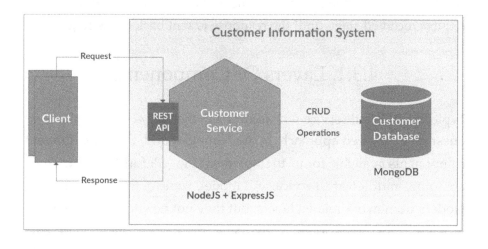

4.3. Low Level Design

SO FAR WE have defined the architecture for the customer information system. Now it's the time to do a deep dive into the low-level design of the API. This step is the next one after the architecture.

In the low-level design, we will go to the API endpoint level design.
After the request has been received by the RESTful service what will
happen to service that request is what we will discuss in the low-level
design of each of the API endpoints. Usually, we will have to create
the sequence diagram for each endpoint at this stage.

Before we jump onto the sequence diagrams it's better to look at
what are all the different components will be involved right from the
request received stage until the response is sent back to the requester.

4.3.1. Layers Or Components

Typically, RESTful service will accomplish the task of serving the request in the layered approach. In the NodeJS world, there are different
components available for us to implement the API functionality. They
are route, middleware, service, and model. Some of them may not be
NodeJS framework related layers, but they not new to the restful service world. In object-oriented languages, the services are most proba-
bly implemented in such a layered approach. We could borrow that
approach here as well.

Below are the different components that we will be using to implement the Customer Service. Let's have a brief look at these components and see what each will do.

1. Controller

Usually, a controller will handle the request, invoke services to perform that action, and process response to sending back to the requester. Often controller will make a sequence of service calls in orchestration to accomplish the request as designed. Technically, it handles the flow of the middleware calls before it sends the response.

2. Middleware

Middleware in a NodeJS world is a function which has access to the request object, response object, and next function. Here the **next()** function is used to invoke the next middleware in the stack.

Middleware functions can perform the following tasks:

1.   Execute any code.
2.   Make changes to the request and the response objects.
3.   End the request-response cycle.
4.   Call the next middleware in the stack.

If the current middleware function does not end the request-response cycle, it must call next() to pass control to the next middleware function. Otherwise, the request will be left hanging.

3. Service

A service is any function which can perform any task, like calculating some formula, accessing database to read or write. Here we will use a service function to access the database for retrieving and storing the customer information.

Also, service will not have access to the request and response object. So anything needs to be done on the request and response object will have to be done in the controller only. Then, the controller will have to pass that information as parameters to the service functions to perform the task. This way there is a clear segregation of duties among all the components in the RESTful service.

4. Model

This component is the data access layer to fetch and save the documents. The service layer will be invoking the models to perform any actions on the document in the database via the model. A model represents the document which can be created, updated, removed and fetched from the database.

4.3.2. Sequence Diagrams

In the above sections, we have gone through all the components/layers we will be engaging to implement the RESTful service. Next step would be to see how can we use these layers to perform each of the functionalities that we defined in the requirements section.

A sequence diagram would be a perfect tool to visualize and describe the flow of the process to develop the code. In this section, we will go through the sequence diagrams for each functionality. This diagram will be very helpful during the development process as it sets the goal of what we are going to develop for those functionalities. With this clear end goal laid out, we can quickly and easily continue with development and testing of the robust API.

1. Add Customer - Sequence Diagram

Below image shows the sequence diagram for the add new customer functionality. As you can see, the request comes to the controller; then it goes through the middleware; finally, it's handled by the model to create the document in the database.

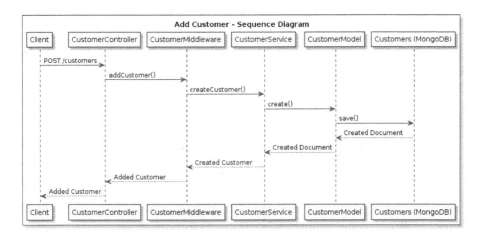

2. Get Customer List - Sequence Diagram

The HTTP GET request will be sent to the controller to get the customers list. The request query parameters will be parsed to extract any searching, filtering and paging information within the controller. Then the list of customers will be retrieved for the search, filter and paging query from the database via the service and model. Finally, the retrieved customer list will be sent back to the requester in the response object.

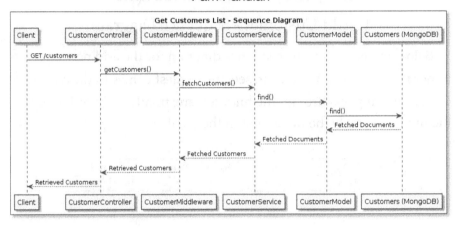

3. Get Customer - Sequence Diagram

What we have here is the sequence diagram for the get a customer functionality. This flow starts with the request comes with the customer id to retrieve the information. As in other sequences, the controller receives the request and retrieves the customer details through the service and model from the database.

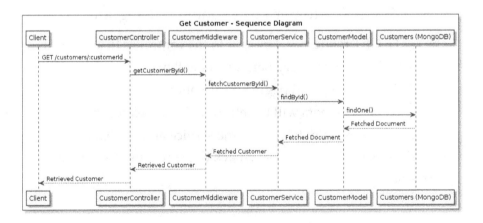

4. Modify Customer - Sequence Diagram

The sequence diagram for modifying a customer functionality is shown here. As per this flow, the request comes with the changed customer details, and the controller handles it. Before the controller responds with the modification result, it invokes the modifyCustomer function in the service. In turn, the model is getting called from the service to make the document update in the database.

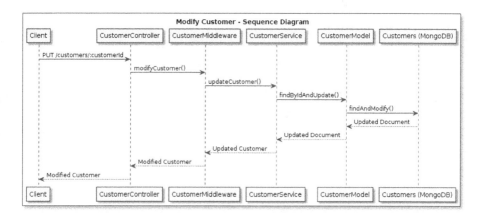

5. Remove Customer - Sequence Diagram

Just like the modify request, the delete a customer request comes with the customer id which needs to be removed from the database. As usual, the controller initiates the process to delete the customer from the database with the help of service and model components.

Parri Pandian

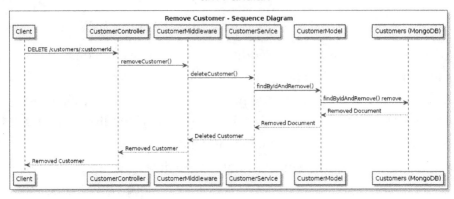

Chapter 5: *Development Environment Setup*

5.1. MongoDB Database Setup

AS WE ARE developing the RESTful service, we need a persistent database to store the data that we create/update via the API. There are many SQL and NoSQL databases available to choose from for the backend for the API. For our API, we can select the MongoDB.

MongoDB is a document database where it stores the data in a flexible JSON-like document format which means fields can vary from document to document and also data structure can be changed over time. Also, there is an excellent wrapper called 'Mongoose' available to make the interaction with MongoDB very easy and straightforward. Mongoose is a MongoDB object modeling for NodeJS.

For development purpose, it's better to install and run the MongoDB locally within the development machine. There are two ways we can get the MongoDB up and running locally.

1. Directly installing and running the MongoDB on the local machine
2. Running MongoDB from the Docker image on the local computer

5.1.1. Install MongoDB Locally

To install the MongoDB on your development machine, you would need to download the MongoDB **community edition** from the MongoDB website https://www.mongodb.com. Follow the installation instruction for the platform (Windows/MacOS/Linux) that you choose to install the MongoDB. Once installed and running, note down the port number as we need to be configured with our NodeJS API.

The steps for installing MongoDB locally, configuring the database and bringing it up would seem cumbersome for some developer. If you are adventurous and won't mind getting your hands dirty, please go ahead and follow the steps as mentioned on the MongoDB website to install and configure it.

For those who want to get the MongoDB up and running quickly without much hassle may want to go with the docker approach as described in the next section.

5.1.2. Running MongoDB On Docker

For a development purpose, I would prefer to bring up the MongoDB on Docker. It's effortless and quick in my opinion. Also, there is an additional benefit of spinning the MongoDB docker image up, which is, you can remove it as soon as you are done with your prototype or development very quickly. This setup will save much space and keep your development machine clean.

Docker is available for many platforms from Windows, MacOS, all flavors of Linux and also for cloud platforms like AWS and Azure. You can download the Docker Community Edition for your operating system and install it.

The latest Docker installer comes with the additional experimental tool called Kitematic which is GUI for managing the docker images and containers.

Once the docker is installed and running, open up the Kitematic and search for 'Mongo'. You will find many public images for Mongo.

I would suggest to pick the official mongo image as shown in the picture and click create. It will download that image locally which you can start to use it right away.

As soon as the image is downloaded, it will start the MongoDB container automatically. Now, note down the access URL as highlighted in the below image. Use this link to access the MongoDB running on the docker. We will use this URL in our NodeJS API to connect to this instance of the MongoDB to create and update the Customer documents.

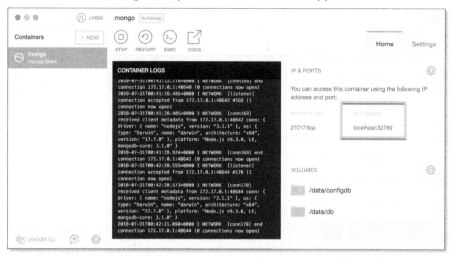

Next step would be to create the module for MongoDB to initialize the connection from the API.

5.2. Base Application Setup

BEFORE WE BEGIN any coding for the API, we need a base application. To set it up, we need to install the Node, Express and other dependent modules as well and create the basic application structure.

5.2.1. Install Node

Go to the Node's website https://nodejs.org and download the NodeJS installer for the platform (Windows/MacOS/Linux) of your choice. The installer comes with NPM (Node Package Manager) module too, which will be needed to install/update further any dependent modules our API codebase and testing scripts would need. You can install either the LTS or Current version of the node on your development machine for this exercise.

Once installed the Node and NPM, you can check each version with below commands.

For Node's version,
```
node --version or node -v
```

For NPM's version,
```
npm --version or npm -v
```

5.2.2. Install Express

For our API development in this book, we will be using the Express web framework for NodeJS. This one is a framework of choice for many API developers as it has various HTTP methods and middleware utilities needed for full-blown API development.

The express module can be installed via npm commands as below. If we try this route, we will have to create the basic application by ourselves from scratch right from the package.json via **npm init** command and other required files and directories.

To install the express module, follow the below steps.

Create a directory for our app and get inside the newly created directory express-service

```
mkdir customer-service
cd customer-service
```

Once changed the working directory, run npm initialization command as below. This command execution will create the package.json file with initial default values. After running this command, it will ask for values to be entered for many attributes of the package.json. Either accept the default value shown for each attribute or enter your choices to complete the initialization.

```
npm init
```

Now is the time to install the express module within your app. With below command, the express module will be added to the package.json as a dependency. Here *--save* is very important as it's the command to let the express module to be added to the package.json file.

```
npm install express --save
```

Next steps will be to create the required files and directories for the base application manually. Although there is a simple step to accomplish this task. The next section will be explaining the quickest way to get the base app up and running.

5.2.3. Install Express Generator & Generate Express App

Instead of creating the express app manually from scratch, we could use the Express Generator tool. This tool will install the express command line tool which you can use to generate the express app skeleton quickly with a single command.

Run the below command to install the Express Generator package. You might need to run this command as the administrator of the machine. This command will install the express generator module globally so that we can execute the *express* command anywhere to create the express app.

```
npm install express-generator -g
```

Once the module has been installed, run the below command to generate the initial express application, and it will come with all the base application features for us to begin.

```
express customer-service
```

In this command, the parameter 'customer-service ' is the app name, and it will create the directory with the same name under the current working directory. In the new app directory, all the express app related files and directories will be automatically created.

Here is the screenshot of the express application created by the *express-generator* tool.

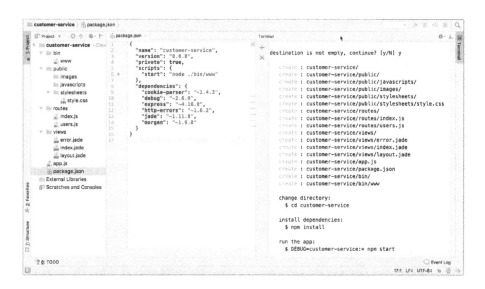

As the output of the above command says, go inside the new app directory and run the *npm install* command to install all the dependencies to be downloaded locally under the *node_modules* directory. This directory will hold all the packages in the dependencies list of the package.json file.

```
cd customer-service
npm install
```

After all of the dependent packages are downloaded, run the below command to start the node server for this app.

```
npm start
```

Now, open a browser and enter the link http://localhost:3000 to verify and confirm the app is running. If it's running, you will be able to view the below page rendered on the browser.

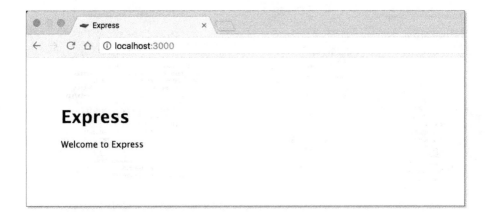

Step 01 - Generated Express Application - Git-Hub

YOU CAN FIND the code that we completed so far in the below Git-Hub repository. Please feel free to check out the whole codebase and explore this step's files in **Step 01 - Generated Express Application** directory.

GitHub Repository:

https://github.com/parripandian/building-nodejs-api-with-tdd-approach

Current Step Directory:

https://github.com/parripandian/building-nodejs-api-with-tdd-approach/tree/master/Step%2001%20-%20Generated%20Express%20Application

5.3. Base Application Preparation

5.2.4. DEEP DIVE Into Generated Express App

So far, we have generated the express app, installed the dependent packages, started the node server for this application and verified that the application is up and running as expected.

Let's dive deeper into the generated base application and see what the files and directories are created. Also, we will review each of this files and directories to understand why they are created by default and its usage.

Let's look at the generated express app's files and directories.

1. bin directory

This directory contains the javascript file *www* which creates the node server and listens to the port **3000**.

2. public directory

It contains few subdirectories: **images, javascript** and **stylesheets** for all own static content files. All the files under this directory will be exposed for public access to serve those static content.

3. routes directory

Routes directory contains some sample routes javascript files. By default, it has **index.js** to render the index page when we access the http://localhost:3000 and **users.js** to demonstrate the resources can be obtained with additional routes configuration.

4. views directory

It is the directory where templates or HTML files can be hosted to serve the static or dynamic content when we use this app as web or mobile application. Express supports various view engines to render the view content. To name a few view engines, Jade, Handlebars Pug and other engines are available for us to use. You can check out the supported view engines with the below command.

```
express -h
```

5. apps.js file

This file is the heart of the express app as all the declaration and initialization of the application is happening here. The **bin/www** file imports and invokes this file to start the node server to render the express application. We will go over this file in details in the further sections.

6. package.json file

This JSON file holds details about the application like name, version, start scripts, test scripts and also the dependencies for deployment and development. *npm* command line utility reads this file to install or update any dependent packages.

7. package-lock.json file

This file keeps the dependency tree installation and its order. As we will add/modify the dependency package and its version over the course of the development process, this file keeps the records of those changes and maintains them. It helps during the subsequent installs by making sure that the packages are installed as described in this dependency tree and in that order.

Now, we have gone over the default content of the generated express app lets clean up the content to make it more relevant for the base app for API development.

5.2.5. Final Preparation Of Base App For API

Express is a flexible web framework, which provides features for complete web and mobile application, with support for both front end and back end features. Since we are using this framework to develop and run the RESTful service, we wouldn't need all the front-end related features like rendering the templates, HTML, stylesheets.

To clean up the express scaffolding app to prepare for our base app, we will have to remove some files, folders and some content from the files.

1. bin directory

This directory is needed as it's the one that creates and runs the server for the RESTful service.

2. public directory

This directory will not be required for the API project as we will not expose any public static content.

3. routes directory

As we will be creating our own routes related files to expose the end-points of the API, we will not need this directory and its content too.

4. views directory

As the API exposes the endpoints it provides for the resources, and it doesn't expose any static content like HTML and templates, we will remove this as well.

5. apps.js file

Even though this file contains both front-end and back-end related modules declarations and initializations, this is needed for the API tool. We will remove those front-end related scripts from this file and make it more robust for the API-only app.js file.

1. Remove the below lines as we removed the routes directory and its content.

```
var indexRouter = require('./routes/index');
var usersRouter = require('./routes/users');

app.use('/', indexRouter);
app.use('/users', usersRouter);
```

2. Remove the below lines as the API will not serve any static content or files.

```
// view engine setup
app.set('views', path.join(__dirname, 'views'));
app.set('view engine', 'jade');

app.use(express.static(path.join(__dirname, 'public')));
```

After removing the above lines if you run the server and navigate to the link http://localhost:3000, you will end up with an error message on the browser along with some error stack trace. That's because of the few more changes needed to be done at the apps.js.

Error: No default engine was specified, and no extension was provided.

Below changes will fix this error message.

1. Remove the below line as it still sends the response as the error page.

```
res.render('error');
```

2. Add the below lines at the same place as the above-removed line. This new lines of code will send the error details as JSON response to the request if and when an error occurred.

```
res.json({
    message: res.locals.message,
```

```
    error: res.locals.error
});
```

3. Also, add the below lines above the error handling code blocks. It is replacing the index page that we just removed with above cleanup task. Essentially this code block is reading from the package.json and sends the information as JSON response to the http://localhost:3000 request.

```
app.get('/', function (req, res) {
    var pkg = require(path.join(__dirname, 'pack-
age.json'));
    res.json({
        name: pkg.name,
        version: pkg.version,
        status: 'up'
    });
});
```

6. package.json file

Since this describes and maintains the app details and dependencies, we will have to keep it intact so that API related details and dependencies are maintained for or reference and npm's need.

Also, we will do some cleanup on this file too. Remove the below line from the dependencies list as we no longer need 'jade' for any view pages response. The versions of these packages could be different when you try this exercise.

```
"jade": "~1.11.0"
```

7. package-lock.json file

This file will be needed for both web & mobile application and RESTful service too. So we will keep this file as it is.

Finally, after all these cleanup tasks and changes are complete if you open up the link http://localhost:3000 in the browser, you will be able to see the below JSON content as per out changes.

With this testing, we are done with the preparation of base app for the API development. We will be using this base app for the further development with API related code.

Step 02 - Final Preparation Of Base App For API - GitHub

YOU CAN FIND the code that we completed so far in the below Git-Hub repository. Please feel free to check out the whole codebase and explore this step's files in **Step 02 - Final Preparation Of Base App For API** directory.

GitHub Repository:

https://github.com/parripandian/building-nodejs-api-with-tdd-approach

Current Step Directory:

https://github.com/parripandian/building-nodejs-api-with-tdd-approach/tree/master/Step%2002%20-%20Final%20Preparation%20Of%20Base%20App%20For%20API

5.4. Application Structure Setup

ONE OF THE factors that either complicate or simplifies the application maintenance over the time is Application Structure. If we get this done correctly, it will be easier to be maintained by the future team that's looking after it. Otherwise, it will become very complicated and cumbersome to do so and also increases the maintenance cost and decreased productivity for further enhancements.

There are many ways for structuring NodeJS app available throughout the internet. Many suggest one approach or the other as each one has pros and cons. In this book, we will be using one of the structure that I have been using for years. This approach gives a more modular structure when the features and modules are increasing over the time and also increases better maintenance of the application.

5.3.1. Modular Approach

For our app, we will follow the below structure. We will be adding below directories in the base application that we prepared in the previous sections.

1. modules directory

In this directory, all the API specific code will be created within their subdirectory. For example, to create the scripts for creating MongoDB connection, we will create 'MongoDB'. Like this, we will also create a directory 'customer' for customer API scripts.

2. tests directory

Since this book's primary goal is to showcase the RESTful service development with the test-driven development approach, we need to maintain the test scripts for all the modules that are developed. So it makes sense to keep the same modular approach for tests scripts as well. This decision will result in creating a directory called '**tests**' along with '**modules**'. Under this tests directory, we will have two more directories too. One directory is for unit testing scripts and another for the integration testing scripts.

One of the best practices is to keep the test data for running the unit and integration tests along with the source code. So we would need one more directory '**fixtures**' for storing any test data for the test scripts.

So, after adding the directories mentioned above, the base app structure will look just like the below image.

▼ 📁 **customer-service** ~/Development/
  ▼ 📁 bin
    📄 www
  ▼ 📁 modules
    📁 customer
    📁 mongodb
  ▶ 📁 node_modules library root
  ▼ 📁 tests
    ▼ 📁 fixtures
      📁 customer
      📁 error
    📁 integration
    ▼ 📁 unit
      📁 customer
      📁 mongodb
  📄 app.js
  📋 package.json
  📋 package-lock.json
📊 External Libraries

Chapter 6: *Development & Testing Setup*

6.1. Apps.js Overview

BEFORE WE BEGIN the code development, we will go over the app-s.js file, and its contents. This javascript is the main file that gets invoked by the server file (bin/www) to start the NodeJS application.

The first few lines in the apps.js are for importing some dependent modules into this file.

```
var createError = require('http-errors');
var express = require('express');
var path = require('path');
var cookieParser = require('cookie-parser');
var logger = require('morgan');
```

We will be using these modules in our app for various reasons which we will go through in the coming sections.

6.1.1. App Level Dependent Modules / Middlewares

Let's go through the modules that are imported in the apps.js. These are used with this file because these dependencies are needed at the app level.

1. express module

This one is the main module for our application as it provides the web application framework packages and also RESTful services related modules like HTTP and other middleware. After a few lines as below, there is an instance created from this module which will be used to describe and define the behavior of the API. Below are the lines that are defining our application.

```
var app = express();
```

Once the instance of the express application is created with the variable app, we will be able to use express application's capabilities to define and shape the RESTful service. Also, this instance of the express application is imported to the server file to start the web server and listened to the port number 3000.

2. morgan module

Morgan is the HTTP logger middleware for NodeJS. With below statement, this logger is mounted onto the express application. This configuration ensures that the HTTP logger is enabled for development environment so that detailed logging will be made for debugging purpose.

```
app.use(logger('dev'));
```

3. body-parser module in the express module

The body-parser module is included with the latest express.js module now. This middleware is used to parse the request body attribute before the request is passed on to other handlers. This object exposes various factories to create the middlewares.

Below statement creates the middleware that parses only the JSON content-type in the request body. After parsing the JSON request body, it creates an object with parsed content and populates the request body attribute with that new object.

```
app.use(express.json());
```

Also, next line in the apps.js adds another body parser middleware which parses only the URL-encoded request bodies and uses the query string library to do so.

```
app.use(express.urlencoded({extended: false}));
```

4. cookie-parser module

To parse the Cookie in the request header, the cookie-parser is used. It populates the req.cookies object with the parsed cookies in key-value pair format with cookie names as keys. The below statement does this parsing and filling the cookie in the express application's request object.

```
app.use(cookieParser());
```

6.1.2. App Base URI Middleware

You might remember from the development environment setup chapter that we added the below block of code within the apps.js file. This code is to handle the express application's base URL http://localhost:3000/.

What we are doing in this code is, we are adding a middleware to handle the base URI '/' and a handler function. It means that whenever the express application encounters the base URI '/' after the server's host and port number or the URL, the following callback function will be invoked.

```
app.get('/', function (req, res) {
    var pkg = require(path.join(__dirname, 'pack-
age.json'));
    res.json({
        name: pkg.name,
        version: pkg.version,
        status: 'up'
    });
});
```

In that callback function, we are reading the **package.json** file content after resolving it's location with the use of Node's **path** utility module. Then the name and version attributes are added to the JSON response object along with the status **'up'** which is to inform the requester that the RESTful service is up and running with the mentioned name and version number.

It's a more straightforward way to send the response to the requester about the RESTful service's necessary information and whether it's up or not. The status attribute may be redundant as the name and version might be more than enough to indicate that service is up. It won't hurt though.

6.1.3. Catch & Throw 404 Not Found Error

Route handlers will be added to process any URI/route. If anyone of the route handlers does not handle any of the routes, the application would have to through 404 error to inform the requester that the resource is not found in the server. To throw the 404 not found error, the below code block is added by the express generator to the apps.js.

```
// catch 404 and forward to error handler
app.use(function (req, res, next) {
    next(createError(404));
});
```

It is a middleware function mounted to the express application. So any request not handled until this code block will be falling through this middleware. A new error object is created and passed on to the next function which in turn invokes the next middleware in the stack. The final middleware in the stack is the Error Handler which is described below.

6.1.4. Error Handling Middleware

We need to handle any error that may occur in the express application and throw the appropriate error message to the requester. Below is error handler code that will be at the end of the apps.js file. The error handler will have four parameters to differentiate from other middlewares.

```
// error handler
app.use(function (err, req, res, next) {
    // set locals, only providing error in development
    res.locals.message = err.message;
    res.locals.error = req.app.get('env') === 'development' ? err : {};

    // render the error page
    res.status(err.status || 500);
```

```
res.json({
    message: res.locals.message,
    error: res.locals.error
});
});
```

This error handler must be added at last after all the app.use(), and routes call to be able to capture and respond when an error occurs with any code before. In this middleware function, the error message and status are prepared and returned as JSON object back to the requester.

6.2. MongoDB Module Setup

LET'S CONTINUE WITH the API codebase now. The API needs to persist the data to the MongoDB database, and since we brought up the MongoDB either by installing and running it locally or by starting it from the docker image, we would still add some scripts within the express application to connect to it when the node server startup.

As we have seen in the modular approach section, we will start writing the mongodb module files in the 'mongodb' directory. Let's create the below files under each directory respectively. Then we will begin filling in with the appropriate scripts.

6.2.1. Module Files Setup

In this section, we will begin with setting up the files needed for mongodb module. Developing the MongoDB connection related scripts will be dealt with in the later part of this section with the TDD approach.

modules/mongodb directory

Under this directory, we will create the below two files for the MongoDB connection related scripts during the application startup.

1.   mongodb.module.js

2.   mongodb.util.js

1. mongodb.module.js file

This one is the main file for mongodb module. It is a unique object exposed as a javascript module. We can use this file to import any other modules declared within this module.

We can start with below code block in this file. It is called **Immediately Invoked Function Expression** (IIFE). I prefer this pattern to enclose the functional code inside the IFFE code block.

It is to restrict the internal variables to be accessible only inside this function and thus it provides privacy to these variables.

```
(function () {

}) ();
```

Next step would be to add the below statement within the IIFE block. What we are doing here is exporting an object via this module. So any types (a function or an object or a literal) will be exposed by this module. Other modules can '**require**' this module to use anything that's revealed by this module to use those.

```
module.exports = {};
```

This the basic structure of the javascript file that we will create in this book. We are declaring this as strict mode as well with the second line.

```
(function () {
    'use strict';

    module.exports = {
```

```
    // Declare attributes here to be exposed to
other modules
    };

})();
```

In short time, we will continue with this file for more functional code along with TDD once we set up other files for this module.

2. mongodb.util.js file

It is where we will create the MongoDB connection creation functional code. The primary content structure will be used for this file as well to begin as below.

```
(function () {
    'use strict';

    module.exports = {
        // Declare attributes here to be exposed to
other modules
    };

})();
```

6.2.2. Test Files Setup

In this section, we will begin with setting up the files needed for testing the mongodb module. We will also go through the dependencies for test scripts and structure of those test script files.

Mocha is the testing framework that we will use here. It provides all the features to construct the unit or integration tests and also to run them. Run the below statement in the command line to include the mocha as a development dependency for this application. It will download and add the mocha library within the project and add the mocha in the package.json file as the development dependency.

```
npm install mocha --save-dev
```

As the unit test needs to assert the actual result of the test is the same as the expected result, we need an assertion library to do so. Chai is one of the best assertion library available for Node. It has both BDD (Behavior Driven Development) and TDD (Test Driven Development) style for assertions. We could use either one of them for our testing. We will use Chai for asserting the test results with BDD assertion style.

```
npm install chai --save-dev
```

It will download and add the chai library within the project and add the chai in the package.json file as the development dependency.

tests/unit/mongodb directory

To write unit tests for the above main files, we will need test files. There are many suggested naming convention for these test specification files. Let's follow one of the naming conventions by prefixing the **.specs** before the **.js** as below. As these are unit test specification files, eventually we place them under **tests/unit** directory for the mongodb module.

1.   mongodb.module.specs.js
2.   mongodb.util.specs.js

As described in the Test Driven Development chapter, we will continue with the mongodb module development in TDD approach.

First, we will write the test scripts for the expected behavior of the functional script and then write minimal code to pass the test that we just wrote. Repeating these steps will eventually result in the completion of the functional scripts in the main javascript files.

1. mongodb.module.spec.js file

To test the mongodb.module.js file, we will use this file. Unit tests for testing the main file's behavior will be written here.

Now, we have the test dependencies added, let's jump onto the test scripts. We need to import or 'require' the assertion library and the BDD style as follows in the mongodb.module.spec.js file.

```
var chai = require('chai');
var expect = chai.expect;
```

We need to set up the test suites further in this file. A bunch of tests can be grouped into a single test suite to run them all at once. In Mocha, we will use the below code block as the test suite.

```
describe('Can be a file/function/module name',
function () {
});
```

The **describe()** contains two parameters: a name and a function that encapsulates the tests. We can also create a nested **describe()** blocks to run a bunch of test suites together.

The scripts that test the behavior of the main file is called **specs** which are shown in the below code.

```
it('should describe the test and it's expectation',
```

```
function () {
});
```

As shown, the spec is defined by its code block, which consists of two parameters like describe, a string and a function. The first parameter can be a brief description of what that spec is testing to confirm the expected behavior of that code block that's being tested.

Inside this specs function, expectations should be defined to compare the actual result with an expected result to test the behavior of the piece of code that's under test. We will use the expect, a BDD style function of the chai assertion library,¬ for building the expectations to assert. Below code is the sample of an expectation.

```
expect(SomeModule).to.be.a('object');
```

So based on the above explanation of the test script file content, here is the **mongodb.module.specs.js** test file's necessary content for the test suite.

```
var chai = require('chai');
var expect = chai.expect;

var MongoDBModule = require('../../../modules/mon-
godb/mongodb.module');

describe('MongoDBModule', function () {

    describe('mongodb.module file', function () {

        it('should test first behavior', function
() {
            // Write expectations here for the be-
havior
        });
```

```
    });


});
```

At the line number 5, we are importing the mongodb.module.js to the test file so that we can test its behavior. Further sections will cover the actual tests we will run through.

2. mongodb.util.spec.js file

To test the mongodb.util.js file, we will use this file. Unit tests for testing the this file's behavior will be written here. Below is the initial content of this file begin with.

```
var chai = require('chai');
var expect = chai.expect;

var MongoDBUtil = require('../../../modules/mon-
godb/mongodb.util');

describe('MongoDBUtil', function () {

    describe('mongodb.util file', function () {

        it('should test first behavior', function
() {
            // Write expectations here for the be-
havior
        });

    });

});
```

6.2.3. MongoDB Configuration File Setup

To make a connection to the MongoDB, we would need to obtain the MongoDB connection parameters in the mongodb.util.js file. We will go over those scripts later in this section. Meanwhile, we could make a configuration file with the conniption details of the MongoDB server.

Below is the configuration file that we will be using for our development. It could be made with environment specific so that different configuration file can be used based on the environment. Anyway, for this book's example, it's out of the scope. Let's continue with the development specific directory and file required for the configuration.

config/mongodb directory

Under the root directory of the application, create a directory **config/mongodb** with a file **mongodb-config.json**. We will be using the JSON format for configuring the MongoDB connection details.

```
{
  "mongodb": {
    "server": "localhost:32769",
    "database": "customer_db_dev",
    "user": null,
    "password": null
  }
}
```

Here, the **server** attribute is the MongoDB URL that you might have noted down during the MongoDB server setup either via direct installation or docker image. The **database** is the name of the database for this RESTful service. If you keep the **user** and **password** attributes as null, you do not need to create the database in the MongoDB server as it will be automatically created when the application is starting up.

6.3. MongoDBModule Unit Tests

WE WILL BEGIN with writing unit test cases for the mongodb.module.js file to test and write the functional code for its expected behavior.

6.3.1. Unit Test 1: Reading MongoDBModule Object

Let's start the first test for the mongodb.module.js file. We want to make sure that the mongodb.module.js file is a module that exposes an object. So we can write the spec like this. This test will be written inside the inner describe() block of the base file content that we just created in the above section.

```
it('should read the mongodb.module file', function
() {
    expect(MongoDBModule).to.be.a('object');
});
```

Since we completed the first test for our codebase, let's run the test suite. To run the test for the whole application we need to add some script in the package.json file. Below is the line that needs to be inserted within the 'scripts' of the package.json file for running the test.

```
"test": "mocha --recursive ./tests"
```

Once it's added, go to the root directory of the application and run the below command in the terminal. It will run the mocha test runner with all the specs available inside the **/tests** directory recursively.

```
npm test
```

Already we have added the functional code in the mongodb.module.js file. So this time the test will run successfully with the one passing test spec as below.

```
> mocha --recursive ./tests


  MongoDBModule
    mongodb.module file
      ✓ should read the mongodb.module file


  1 passing (7ms)
```

6.3.2. Unit Test 2: Reading MongoDBUtil Object

The purpose of the mongodb.module.js file is to expose all of its files. So that we don't have to 'require' any of this module's files separately in other modules' files wherever needed. So far, we have one another file mongodb.util.js file along with this file.

Test Script

Next step would be to add a spec in this test file to read the MongoDBUtil object via the MongoDBModule object. For this, the following **it()** block with that specific expectation would be appropriate to go with.

```
it('should confirm MongoDBUtil exist', function ()
{
    expect(MongoDBModule.MongoDBUtil).to.be.a('ob-
ject');
});
```

The spec is defined to expect the attribute MongoDBUtil of the MongoDBModule object is an object type just like any module file. This way we are confirming that MongoDBUtil attribute is existing in the MongoDBModule object.

If we run the mocha test now, we will eventually get the new test failed. Below is the screenshot of the test run with the current state of the javascript files.

```
MongoDBModule
  mongodb.module file
    ✓ should read the mongodb.module file
    1) should confirm MongoDBUtil exist


1 passing (10ms)
1 failing

1) MongoDBModule
     mongodb.module file
       should confirm MongoDBUtil exist:
    AssertionError: expected undefined to be an object
      at Context.<anonymous> (tests/unit/mongodb/mongodb.module.spec.js:15:53)
```

As per TDD, we are on the right track now. We just wrote a failing unit test. The next step would be to write minimal code in the mongodb.module.js to make this test pass.

Code

Since this test is expecting an attribute MongoDBUtil in the MongoDBModule object, we can accomplish this expectation with the below code added within the **module.exports** object block in the mongodb.module.js file.

```
MongoDBUtil: require('./mongodb.util')
```

Let's run the test once again, and this time it will pass as we just added the code for the spec's expectation. Following is the passing tests screenshot.

```
MongoDBModule
  mongodb.module file
    ✓  should read the mongodb.module file
    ✓  should confirm MongoDBUtil exist


2 passing (8ms)
```

We got the second test run successfully. To abide by the TDD philosophy, let's see what we can do to refactor the code if there is an opportunity. By looking at the mongodb.module.js, there is not much we do to refactor it. So we can leave it as it is for now.

Although there is no need to refactor the main javascript file, there is one little thing we can to do in the mongodb.util.spec.js file, which is the test suite for the mongodb.util.js file. You may have noticed in the mongodb.util.spec.js file that we **require** the mongodb.util.js directly.

```
var MongoDBUtil = require('../../../modules/mon-
```

```
godb/mongodb.util');
```

As we have seen in the above section, the main purpose of the mongodb.module.js file is to expose all other files that belong to the module. So it would be appropriate to refactor the line as mentioned earlier as below. What we are doing here is getting the MongoDBUtil object via the mongodb.module.js file.

```
var MongoDBUtil = require('../../../modules/mongodb/mongodb.module').MongoDBUtil;
```

Rerunning the mocha test runner will make all the existing specs to pass successfully as we just refactored the scripts without changing any of the behavior of the functional code base.

6.4. MongoDBUtil Unit Tests

WE WILL CONTINUE with writing unit test cases for the mongodb.util.js file to test and write the functional code for its expected behavior.

6.4.1. Unit Test 3: Reading MongoDBUtil Object

Just like the Unit Test 1 for the MongoDBModule, we could write the same spec for the mongodb.util.js file as well. In this test, MongoDBUtil will be expected to be an object.

```
it('should read the mongodb.module file', function
() {
    expect(MongoDBUtil).to.be.a('object');
});
```

Below will be the test result, and it will successfully be running the three specs that we wrote so far.

```
MongoDBModule
  mongodb.module file
    ✓   should read the mongodb.module file
    ✓   should confirm MongoDBUtil exist

MongoDBUtil
  mongodb.util file
    ✓   should read the mongodb.util file


3 passing (7ms)
```

6.4.2. Unit Test 4: Initializing MongoDB Connection

So far we have covered the basic test suites for both the javascript files. The fundamental reason for this module is to initialize the MongoDB connection while the application is starting up. This test will cover this functionality/behavior.

Even though we could write a unit test for testing the MongoDB connection initialization code block, somehow I am not able to mock or stub the mongoose library related objects and functions and also not able to assert the result of the connection with the spec. If you can get this unit tested, please let me know, will include that in this book.

Test Script

So, for the connection initialization behavior, we will write the spec to check that there is an **init** function that takes care of the MongoDB connection within itself. Also, we will write the complete required script in the module.util.js file for which we will not have any expectation written in the spec.

```
it('should confirm init function exist', function
() {
    expect(MongoDBUtil.init).to.be.a('function');
});
```

Moreover, this re-running the mocha test will show one error as shown in the below picture as the new spec didn't pass.

```
1) MongoDBUtil
     mongodb.util file
        should confirm init function exist:
     AssertionError: expected undefined to be a function
       at Context.<anonymous> (tests/unit/mongodb/mongodb.util.spec.js:15:44)
```

Code

We will have to add the code block in the mongodb.util.js file so that all the tests will pass again.

```
module.exports = {
    init: init
};

function init() {
}
```

Let's fill in this **init()** function with the actual code in just a while.

Meantime, let's try to make running the mocha tests automatic. As we cannot keep running the **npm test** command manually every time we change some code in the module files. We could save time if the tests run whenever there is a change in the javascript. It could be achieved by updating a line in the package.json file.

Replace the below in the package.json file,

```
"test": "mocha --recursive ./tests"
```

With the below line.

```
"test": "mocha --recursive ./tests --watch ./modules"
```

By merely adding **--watch** with the modules directory as additional parameter to the **mocha** command, we are instructing the mocha test runner to keep a watch on the files under the modules directory, and it will run the test suites whenever there is any change in the javascript files.

After applying the above changes, once changing any of the code will trigger the tests automatically and will show whether that change affected the test suites or not either passing or failing the tests.

Here are the test results so far for the MongoDB module files.

```
MongoDBModule
  mongodb.module file
    ✓  should read the mongodb.module file
    ✓  should confirm MongoDBUtil exist

MongoDBUtil
  mongodb.util file
    ✓  should read the mongodb.util file
    ✓  should confirm init function exist


4 passing (24ms)
```

6.5. MongoDB Connection Initialization

NOW, LET'S START with the code development for making MongoDB connection. We would be using the Mongoose library to handle
the MongoDB connection and query interactions.

This MongoDB object modeling for NodeJS library provides a
schema-based solution for defining the model for our application
data. It also offers in-built typecasting, validation, query building and
business logic hooks along with more features.

Using this library will be making the developer's life a little bit easy
during the development as it abstracts the low-level MongoDB APIs
and provides many user-friendly methods to handle the interaction
with the MongoDB database.

1. Download Dependencies

As usual, we will start downloading and adding the Mongoose
module as a dependent in the package.json file with the below command.

```
npm install mongoose --save
```

Also, the MongoDB module.

```
npm install mongodb --save
```

Once the two modules are downloaded into the **node_modules** directory, which is where the npm utility will download all the dependent
modules from the www.npmjs.com and keep them locally for the application's use, let's continue with the adding more scripts in the
mongodb.util.js file.

2. Load Required Modules/Files

Load the mongoose module with the below statement, by requiring
it, just below the **module.exports** block.

```
var mongoose = require('mongoose');
```

Also, the MongoDB configuration needs to be loaded in this file so
that we could get the mongodb connection details.

```
var mongodbConfig = require('../../config/mongodb/
mongodb-config').mongodb;
```

3. Connect To MongoDB Database

Connection to the MongoDB can be made with the **mongoose.con-
nect()** method. This method needs connection URI as a mandatory
first parameter and options object as an optional second parameter.
Also, it can accept a callback function as an optional parameter at the
end.

```
mongodb.connect(uri, options, callbackFunction)
```

If we don't pass the callback function while connecting, the connect method will return a promise, which we could handle in the calling function. Below will be the method for the promise return.

```
mongodb.connect(uri, options)
```

We will use the promise function so that we could add appropriate handling functions for success and failure of the promise.

4. Prepare Connection URI

As we have the MongoDB database details in the JSON configuration file, we will have prepared the connection URI as per the prescribed format to pass it to the mongoose.connect() function.

Below is the standard MongoDB connection URI format to connect to the MongoDB database.

```
mongodb://username:password@host:port/database?op-
tions
```

Let's break this string to see what are the different components and their role in the below section.

1. **mongodb://**: This is the required prefix which identifies that this is a string in the standard connection URI format.
2. **username:password@**: This is an optional string. When specified, the client will be logging into the database with this credential after the connection to the MongoDB server is established. If this is not specified, the client will be logging into the database anonymously.
3. **host**: This is the MongoDB server address, and it could be a hostname, IP address or UNIX domain socket.
4. **:port**: The port number of the MongoDB database server and is

optional.

5. **/database**: The name of the database that we want to connect to in the MongoDB server, and this is also an optional parameter.

6. **?options**: Connection-specific options. We will use one or two of these options within this example.

The MongoDB connection details are in the JSON file, and we need to use that information to format the connection URI. So we will create a new function inside the mongodb.util.js for preparing the connection URI from the configuration JSON file.

```
function prepareConnectionString(config) {
    var connectionString = 'mongodb://';

    if (config.user) {
        connectionString += config.user + ':' + con-
fig.password + '@';
    }

    connectionString += config.server + '/' + con-
fig.database;

    return connectionString;
}
```

This function receives the input of config object which contains the connection details and returns the connection URI as the response. Inside this function, connection URI is prepared as per the standard format as described in the above section. If the user and password are available in the config object, the credential is added to the connection string otherwise omitted.

5. Complete Init Function

Let's continue with updating the init function with database connection code. Now we know the mongoose method to connect to the
MongoDB database and its inputs. We already have the function to
prepare the connection URI from the config object, so lets complete
the init function.

Inside the init function, let's create two variables: one for options
and another one for the connection string. Also, then call the mon-
goose.connect() function with those inputs and handle the promise
functions for both success and failure.

```
function init() {
    var options = {
        promiseLibrary: require('bluebird'),
        useNewUrlParser: true
    };

    var connectionString =
prepareConnectionString(mongodbConfig);

    mongoose.connect(connectionString, options)
        .then(function (result) {
            console.log("MongoDB connection suc-
cessful. DB: " + connectionString);
        })
        .catch(function (error) {
            console.log(error.message);
            console.log("Error occurred while con-
necting to DB: : " + connectionString);
        });
}
```

For the options object, let's add **bluebird** promise library that can be used by the mongoose module to throw the promises as required. So we need to add the bluebird module into the dependencies list with the below command.

```
npm install bluebird --save
```

To format the connection URI, we will use the new function **prepare-ConnectionString()** that we created a while back by passing the MongoDB config object we loaded at the beginning of this file.

Since we are using the mongoose.connect() without the callback function, means, using the promise version of it, we need to handle the promise. So, we pass a function to then function as input to handle the successful connection. Also passed another function to the catch function to handle any connection failure. Inside each of those handler functions, we print the appropriate messages to the console for debugging purpose.

Even after these changes in the mongodb.util.js file, the test suites should still run without any failures.

As we have completed the whole MongoDB module with required functionality changes, let's invoke the init function from the app.js to initialize the MongoDB connection during the application startup.

So let's load the MongoDBUtil from the MongoDBModule in the apps.js, just below the initial load of all the app level dependent modules.

```
var MongoDBUtil = require('./modules/mongodb/mon-
godb.module').MongoDBUtil;
```

Just below the app.use() of all other modules in the apps.js, add the below line to invoke the init function for initializing the MongoDB connection.

```
MongoDBUtil.init();
```

This statement completes the MongoDB module. Restarting the application with *npm start* will make the database connection while the application is starting up. Either database connection success or failure message will be displayed at the console once the server is up and running.

```
MongoDB connection successful. DB: mongodb://localhost:32769/customer_db_dev
[]
```

Step 03 - MongoDB Module Setup - GitHub

YOU CAN FIND the code that we completed so far in the below Git-Hub repository. Please feel free to check out the whole codebase and explore this step's files in **Step 03 - MongoDB Module Setup** directory.

GitHub Repository:

https://github.com/parripandian/building-nodejs-api-with-tdd-approach

Current Step Directory:

https://github.com/parripandian/building-nodejs-api-with-tdd-approach/tree/master/Step%2003%20-%20MongoDB%20Module%20Setup

6.6. Customer Module Setup

NOW LET'S START with the customer module. In this module, we will write the functional code needed for our API. We will apply the Test Driven Development approach to develop every piece of code to accomplish the task. Just like the previous module, we will begin by setting up the directories and files for the module. Also the initial code for each of those files as per each one's type.

6.6.1. Module Files Setup

As we have already set up the customer directory (**modules/customer**) in the Development Environment Setup chapter, let's create the below list of files in the same directory and we will go over these files and why we need those files in the following sections.

1. customer.module.js
2. customer.controller.js
3. customer.middleware.js
4. customer.service.js
5. customer.model.js

1. customer.module.js file

It is the main file for the customer module which will be used by other modules to get the reference for this module's files. So that other modules will have to load only this file instead of few or all the files as needed.

There is one difference between this module file and the previous mongodb module file. This file will load a function to the module object. The reason is, as this file will be loaded within other files of this module to get the handle for rest of the files.

So it needs to be exposing a function which will return an object with all other files as an attribute upon calling this function. We will see in action why we need this file to be a function loaded as module object while developing this file with more functionalities.

2. customer.controller.js file

The entry point for any request will be this file. As it will expose the Router object to as the module object which will route the requests as defined in this object. Routing means how the application responds to the client request to a particular endpoint (URI or path) and a specific HTTP method (GET, POST, PUT or DELETE).

The URI for all the endpoints will be defined in this file along with one or more handler functions. So when a request's URI matches any of the route definitions will be handled by the handlers associated with the route definition.

Each route definition will have a final handler to process the result from the other previous handler functions and send the response back to the client. The handler functions could be a middleware function which has access to request, response objects and next function. So the request will cascade through these handler functions and finally return the response object with the result as per the request.

3. customer.middleware.js file

To handle the customer related paths or URIs, we will create the middleware functions in this file. As you know already, middleware functions have access to the request, response objects and next function to invoke other middleware functions in the stack.

One of the primary purposes of the middleware is to change the request and response objects as needed. So, this file's middleware functions will read the required query, parameters and body objects from the request and call the functions of the service files to execute the code necessary to accomplish the requested task. Once the code execution is complete and appropriate result has been obtained, the middleware could end the request-response cycle after placing the result in the response object to be sent to the client.

If there are different tasks need to be completed for the request as per the middleware functions associated with the path in the routing definition, next middlewares will be invoked to perform their tasks. While doing so, these middlewares can place some data in the request object to share the data across the middlewares in the stack. The last middleware in the stack would end the request-response cycle unless there is no error thrown the any of the previous middlewares.

4. customer.service.js file

Even though the middleware functions can directly interact with the file systems / databases to add / modify / fetch the data, it would clutter the middleware function as it would end up doing more than one thing unnecessarily. We could offload the file system / database interaction to another file which we can call service.

This way we can keep the lines of code in each of these files' functions as less as possible to make it more readable and maintainable.

By doing so, will also make it more modular. Another benefit we could get from this approach is that the middleware will have to parse the request object to extract the required information to be passed to the service functions and also deal with the response objects as well. Also, the service functions will not have access to the request and response objects but the required information which is passed as the parameters.

5. customer.model.js file

Since we use MongoDB document database for storing the customer information, we need to define the shape of the document. It is the file where we specify the properties of the customer document and its datatypes.

We will need the mongoose to handle all the MongoDB related interaction. In mongoose, everything starts with the definition of the Schema for the data that we want to store in the MongoDB collection. The schema defines the shape of the document, and it's compiled to create the Model class for the customer details. The instance of the Customer Model class is the one that we store in the collection as a Customer Document.

In this file, the Customer Model class is exported as a module, and it's used to create, update, delete and fetch the customer documents in the MongoDB database.

6.6.2. Segregation of Duties

With these different files, there is a clear segregation of duties are well defined as below.

1. **customer.module.js:** Main javascript file where all the module files are exposed as attributes in the object which can be used

to load each file in other modules' files.

2. **customer.controller.js:** This is an express router exposed as a function with the router for each path or URI is well defined along with handler middleware functions. Request to a particular endpoint is handled here with appropriate routing to serve that request.

3. **customer.middleware.js:** Handling of request and response objects are performed at this file. Also, the requested action is accomplished within each of the middleware functions by calling service functions with required parameters which are extracted from the request object at this layer.

4. **customer.service.js:** The functions available in this file deal with the actions for creating, updating deleting and fetching the document through the Model. It is an intermediary between the controller and model to preprocess the documents for the required operation.

5. **customer.model.js:** The interaction between then MongoDB is happening here with the help of mongoose module. All the document creation, updating, deletion and retrieval from the database is handled by the models which are exported as the module by this file.

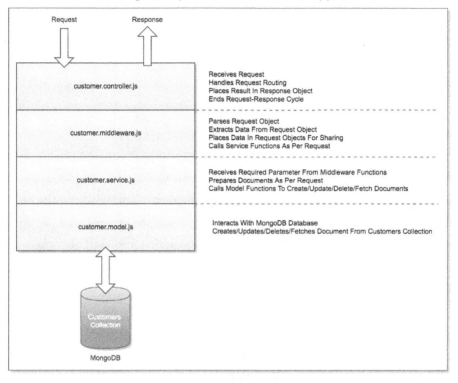

6.6.3. Test Files Setup

For the files available in this module, we will create the spec files. Although, we won't be writing any unit test scripts for the controller and model files. Like unit testing, the model file may not be needed as we will be adding required tests in the service spec itself.

Also for the controller file, we may not be successfully able to write the specs to test it's behavior with appropriate mocking or stubbing the dependent functions. However, we will be writing integration test specs in the coming chapter which will be examining the behavior of the controller file itself along with all the files in the layers as a whole.

So, for now, below test files will be created under the tests/unit/

customer directory.

1. customer.module.spec.js
2. customer.middleware.spec.js
3. customer.service.spec.js

6.6.4. Test Fixtures Setup

While we test the functionality with the unit test scripts, we would eventually use a sample data set to pass as inputs and confirm the outputs. We could create these data inside the specs themselves. However, this approach will clutter the test script and will become cumbersome to maintain it if the testing data grows more substantial over the time.

There is a way to avoid this issue and keep the file clean for only the testing scripts. The test data can be maintained outside of the specs and loaded whenever it's needed upon running the test. The files that hold the test data is called fixtures. As we will be writing the API code for almost all the HTTP methods, the input and output data will become more than we want to maintain the each of the spec itself.

We will create these files with empty JSON format ({ }) for now and fill in with appropriate content in JSON format while we go through each of the tests. So below are the fixtures that we would need for the testing. Let's create these files in the **tests/fixtures** directory. All the files mentioned below will have to have only the empty JSON format with just { } string as content.

tests/fixtures/customer directory

These files contain the test data needed for the customer module files testing.

1. new-customer.json

2.   created-customer.json

3.   modified-customer.json

4.   customers.json

tests/fixtures/error directory

Since we will also test the negative test scenarios with error thrown from any of the layer, error related test data will be required as well. Content for these files will also be filled in the coming sections.

1.   error-404.json

2.   error-unknown.json

Fixture Scripts

Apart from the JSON files, we will need a few more javascript files which will be exposing these test files as attributes of an object. So that we can avoid requiring individual files separately with its full path wherever it's needed. Just like the mongodb.module file lets create the below files under the specified directories as below.

1.   tests/fixtures/customer/customer-fixture.js

2.   tests/fixtures/error/error-fixture.js

3.   tests/fixtures/fixtures.js

1. tests/fixtures/customer/customer-fixture.js file

This file will expose all the test fixtures from the tests/fixtures/customer/ directory. The content of this file will be as follows.

```
(function () {
    'use strict';
```

```
module.exports = {
    customers: require('./customers.json'),
    newCustomer: require('./new-
customer.json'),
    createdCustomer: require('./created-cus-
tomer.json'),
    modifiedCustomer: require('./modified-cus-
tomer.json')
    };

})();
```

2. tests/fixtures/error/error-fixture.js file

To expose error related test fixtures from the tests/fixtures/error/ directory, we will use this file with the below content.

```
(function () {
    'use strict';

    module.exports = {
        unknownError: require('./error-unknown.j-
son'),
        error404: require('./error-404.json')
    };

})();
```

3. tests/fixtures/fixtures.js file

Finally, as might be adding more modules for the API, the number of fixtures javascript files will also be increased. So we might end up requiring these javascript files with their full path in the respective test module files. We could even make this simpler by creating another high-level fixture javascript files to expose all the module level fixture javascript files. The fixtures.js file under the tests/fixtures will be used for that purpose.

Here is the content of this file which exposes the attributes with the appropriate module level fixture javascript files for quick and easy access to the need to know those files' complete path.

```
(function () {
    'use strict';

    module.exports = {
        CustomerFixture: require('./customer/cus-
tomer-fixture'),
        ErrorFixture: require('./error/error-fix-
ture')
    };

})();
```

Here is the content of this file. With this, we have completed all the test fixtures that we would need for all the specs of this RESTful Service. Now, we will start with some initial specs for the customer module, and we will add more tests as we go further.

6.7. CustomerModule Unit Tests

THIS SECTION CONTAINS all the unit test cases for the customer.-module.js file to test and write the functional code for it's expected behavior.

6.7.1. Unit Test 5: Reading CustomerModule Function

As a first test, we will start with the customer.module.js file where we will test for the CustomerModule function which is exposed as a module.

Test Script

Let's add the initial test file content in the customer.module.spec.js file. With chai and expect modules loaded at the beginning, the main test suite is added as below. We are loading the custom.module.js file into a variable CustomerModule by requiring that javascript file.

```
var chai = require('chai');
var expect = chai.expect;

var CustomerModule = require('../../../modules/cus-
tomer/customer.module');
```

```
describe('CustomerModule', function () {

});
```

Inside this test suite, we will add the new test suite to test the CustomerModule function. Since we already loaded the module file, let's write a spec that will expect for the CustomerModule to be a function.

```
describe('customer.module file', function () {
 it('should confirm CustomerModule function exist',
function () {
        expect(CustomerModule).to.be.a('function');
   });
});
```

If we run the mocha test runner now, it will show one unit test failure as we haven't written anything in the customer.module.js yet.

```
1) CustomerModule
     customer.module file
       should confirm CustomerModule function exist:
     AssertionError: expected {} to be a function
       at Context.<anonymous> (tests/unit/customer/customer.module.spec.js:10:42)
```

Code

To make the above spec to pass, we will develop the expected behavior which is the module should be returning a function. As usual, we will start with the initial javascript content which is an IIFE code block. Also, create an empty function called 'init' and assign it to the **module.exports** statement. This statement will expose the init function as a module for the customer.module.js file.

```
(function () {
```

```
'use strict';

module.exports = init;

function init() {
}
```

```
})();
```

As we have written the minimal code that satisfies the expectation of the spec that we just wrote, running the unit test will result in all the passing test suites.

```
CustomerModule
  customer.module file
    ✓   should confirm CustomerModule function exist
```

6.7.2. Unit Test 6: CustomerModule Function Returns Object

Continuation of the above test, we will add one more spec to test that the CustomerModule function returns an object. This function is where will add the attributes for the rest of the files in this modules.

Test Script

Below is the spec with the expectation of the CustomerModule function to return an object when it's called. Add this spec just below the first spec in the customer.module.spec.js file.

```
it('should confirm CustomerModule function returns
an object', function () {
```

112

```
expect(CustomerModule()).to.be.a('object');
});
```

If we run the mocha test runner now, it will show one unit test failure as we haven't written any code for the current test case in the customer.module.js yet.

```
1) CustomerModule
     customer.module file
        should confirm CustomerModule function returns an object:
     AssertionError: expected undefined to be an object
       at Context.<anonymous> (tests/unit/customer/customer.module.spec.js:14:44)
```

Code

For making the CustomerModule function to return the object as a result, we need to make the init function in the customer.module.js to return an object as this is the function exposed with the module. Below is the update code for the init function to meet the spec's expectation. It will make the new test to pass successfully.

```
function init() {
    return {}
}
```

As we have written the minimal code that satisfies the expectation of the spec that we just wrote, running the unit test will result in all the passing test suites.

```
CustomerModule
  customer.module file
    ✓   should confirm CustomerModule function exist
    ✓   should confirm CustomerModule function returns an object
```

6.7.3. Unit Test 7: Reading CustomerController Function

Next spec that we are going to write will test for the CustomerController attribute which is part of the CustomerModule function's returned object.

Test Script

As mentioned above, this test will be calling the CustomerModule function and expecting that the CustomerController attribute of function type which will be part of the response.

```
it('should confirm CustomerController function ex-
ist', function () {

expect(CustomerModule().CustomerController).to.be.a
('function');

});
```

Running the test suites will yield an error as the test result as shown in the below screenshot.

```
1) CustomerModule
    customer.module file
        should confirm CustomerController function exist:
    AssertionError: expected undefined to be a function
        at Context.<anonymous> (tests/unit/customer/customer.module.spec.js:18:63)
```

Code

This test requires changes in two files: customer.controller.js and customer.module.js.

As explained at the beginning of this section, CustomerController will expose the Router object which is part of the ExpressJS framework. To make this test pass, let's add the below code block in the **customer.controller.js**.

```
(function () {
    'use strict';

    var express = require('express');
    var router = express.Router();

    module.exports = router;

})();
```

What we are doing here is, we are creating a router object from the express module and exporting it by assigning to the module.exports object. So, when this file is loaded to any variable in other files, it will load the router object itself.

Here is the next change needed for making that spec to pass. In the response object of the customer.module.js file, we need to add an attribute which loads the customer.controller.js file by requiring it. It will pass the latest spec as it satisfies the expectation.

```
function init() {
    return {
        CustomerController: require('./customer.-
controller')
    }
}
```

As shown in the below screenshot, the latest unit test will be passing successfully now.

```
CustomerModule
  customer.module file
    ✓ should confirm CustomerModule function exist
    ✓ should confirm CustomerModule function returns an object
    ✓ should confirm CustomerController function exist
```

6.7.4. Unit Test 8: Reading CustomerMiddleware Object

Just like the above test, we can add a new spec to test the CustomerMiddleware object from the CustomerModule call.

Test Script

Below is the spec for testing the CustomerMiddleware object.

```
it('should confirm CustomerMiddleware object
exist', function ()   {
                expect(CustomerModule().Cus-
tomerMiddleware).to.be.a('object');
});
```

This test script will be causing the below error as the functional code to satisfy this test case is not yet written.

```
1) CustomerModule
     customer.module file
       should confirm CustomerMiddleware object exist:
     AssertionError: expected undefined to be an object
       at Context.<anonymous> (tests/unit/customer/customer.module.spec.js:22:63)
```

Code

This spec also warrants changes in two files: customer.middleware.js and customer.module.js. As the changes in the first file exports an object and latter file exposes that object through an attribute CustomerMiddleware.

Here is the code for the customer.middleware.js. It is the basic functional code for the module file as we have seen in the earlier chapter.

```
(function () {
    'use strict';

    module.exports = {};

})();
```

We will add the below line in the init function's response object in the customer.module.js file, just below the CustomerController attribute.

```
CustomerMiddleware: require('./
customer.middleware')
```

Add the necessary comma at the end of each attribute's declaration to avoid any javascript error. We will get the spec for this functional code passed when we run the mocha test runner.

```
CustomerModule
  customer.module file
    ✓  should confirm CustomerModule function exist
    ✓  should confirm CustomerModule function returns an object
    ✓  should confirm CustomerController function exist
    ✓  should confirm CustomerMiddleware object exist
```

6.7.5. Unit Test 9: Reading CustomerService Object

This test is testing the CustomerService object returned as one of the attributes of the CustomerModule function call.

Test Script

Below is the spec for testing the CustomerService object.

```
it('should confirm CustomerService object exist',
function () {

expect(CustomerModule().CustomerService).to.be.a('o
bject');
});
```

This test script will be causing the below error as the functional code to satisfy this test case is not yet written.

```
1) CustomerModule
     customer.module file
        should confirm CustomerService object exist:
      AssertionError: expected undefined to be an object
        at Context.<anonymous> (tests/unit/customer/customer.module.spec.js:26:60)
```

Code

Both customer.service.js and customer.module.js files need to be updated for this test as well. We will update the customer.service.js with the essential javascript content just like the customer.middleware.js as it needs to export an object.

```
(function () {
    'use strict';

    module.exports = {};

})();
```

Also, let's update the customer.module.js file's init function with the below line in the response object.

```
CustomerService: require('./customer.service')
```

Just like the other specs, this one will also run successfully now while testing.

```
CustomerModule
  customer.module file
    ✓  should confirm CustomerModule function exist
    ✓  should confirm CustomerModule function returns an object
    ✓  should confirm CustomerController function exist
    ✓  should confirm CustomerMiddleware object exist
    ✓  should confirm CustomerService object exist
```

6.7.6. Unit Test 10: Reading CustomerModel Function

Finally, we have come to the last spec of this section. Here we will test for the CustomerModel function.

Test Script

Below is the spec for testing the CustomerModel object when calling the CustomerModule function.

```
it('should confirm CustomerModel function exist',
function () {

expect(CustomerModule().CustomerModel).to.be.a('fun
ction');
});
```

Running the test suites will yield an error as the test result as shown in the below screenshot.

```
1) CustomerModule
     customer.module file
       should confirm CustomerModel function exist:
     AssertionError: expected undefined to be a function
       at Context.<anonymous> (tests/unit/customer/customer.module.spec.js:30:58)
```

Code

CustomerModel is the class definition which is compiled from the Mongoose's Schema definition. Customer document in the MongoDB database is the instance of the CustomerModel. The schema for the customer maps to the Customers MongoDB collection and defines the shape of the customer documents within that collection.

At first, we will load the mongoose module to start with for defining the CustomerModel in the default IIFE code block as below. From the mongoose, we need to get the Schema constructor which will be used to define the CustomerSchema with required attributes for the customer document.

Below is the complete content of the customer.model.js file.

```javascript
(function () {
    var mongoose = require('mongoose');

    var Schema = mongoose.Schema;

    var CustomerSchema = new Schema({
        firstName: {
            type: String,
            required: true
        },
        lastName: {
            type: String,
            required: true
        },
        email: {
            type: String,
            required: true
        },
        phoneNumber: {
            type: Number,
            required: true
        },
        address: String,
        city: String,
        state: String,
        zipCode: String,
        country: String
    });

    module.exports = mongoose.model('customers',
CustomerSchema);
```

```
}) ();
```

The attributes are defined in the schema as per the requirement specification of the customer details that we have seen in the requirements
chapter. Each attribute is specified with the type of SchemaType available in the mongoose.

Below is the permitted SchemaTypes with which we can assign the
attribute's type.

1. String
2. Number
3. Date
4. Buffer
5. Boolean
6. Mixed
7. ObjectId
8. Array

We can also declare whether the attribute is required or not required with the 'required' flag. When an attribute is declared with required as true, if we save the document without that particular attribute, MongoDB will throw an exception of missing attribute. This
flag will enforce the validation of that attribute's availability in the
document while saving in the database.

Once the structure of the document is defined with the Schema constructor with all the attributes, we need to compile it to make a Model
out of it. The below line does the compilation of the Schema to create
the Model.

```
module.exports = mongoose.model('customers', Cus-
tomerSchema);
```

What happens with this line is, mongoose.model() is copying the

Schema definition and provides an interface to the MongoDB collection called 'customers' which is the first parameter of this function. This model will be used to create document instances.

If we pass the first parameter, the collection name, as the singular form, Mongoose will convert to the plural form of the collection name while it creates it in the MongoDB. Preferably, always try to use the plural form for the collection name to avoid any automatic conversion issue.

The above statement will be returning the Model constructor of function type. We are assigning the function to the module.exports object. This assignment will satisfy the specs' expectation of a function type to be returned for the CustomerModule().CustomerModel statement after the next described change.

The second change for this spec is to be done in the customer.module.js file where the CustomerModel attribute will be loaded with the customer.model.js file as below.

```
CustomerModel: require('./customer.model')
```

With this line of code, we have completed the test suite for the customer.module.js file. Below is the mocha test result for this module's test suite. All the specs should be running successfully.

```
CustomerModule
  customer.module file
    ✓ should confirm CustomerModule function exist
    ✓ should confirm CustomerModule function returns an object
    ✓ should confirm CustomerController function exist
    ✓ should confirm CustomerMiddleware object exist
    ✓ should confirm CustomerService object exist
    ✓ should confirm CustomerModel function exist
```

Step 04 - Customer Module Setup - GitHub

YOU CAN FIND the code that we completed so far in the below Git-Hub repository. Please feel free to check out the whole codebase and explore this step's files in the **Step 04 - Customer Module Setup** directory.

GitHub Repository:

https://github.com/parripandian/building-nodejs-api-with-tdd-approach

Current Step Directory:

https://github.com/parripandian/building-nodejs-api-with-tdd-approach/tree/master/Step%2004%20-%20Customer%20Module%20Setup

PART THREE: Developing & Testing the REST API

Chapter 7: *Add Customer API*

7.1. Add Customer Functionality

SO FAR, WE have set up the module and test files with an initial set of test suites and functional code implemented successfully. Now it's the time for developing the required functionalities as per the requirement specifications laid down in the earlier chapter.

7.2. CustomerService - Create Customer Unit Tests

IN THIS SECTION, we will start with writing test scripts and coding the required functional script for the CustomerService module file.

7.2.1. CustomerService Spec File Preparation

We will start by preparing the customer.service.spec.js file with the initial content needed for test suites.

1. Load Required Test Modules

Here is the first content for this test file where the list of test related modules is necessary for the specs is loaded.

```
'use strict';

var chai = require('chai');
var expect = chai.expect;
var sinon = require('sinon');

var mongoose = require('mongoose');
```

You are already aware of the first two modules that are loaded here as we have used them in the previous modules. The last one, Sinon, is new here. We will be using Sinon for creating spies, stubs and mocks while testing the unit of code. Let's look at what are these and when to use them.

What is a Test Spy?

A test spy is a function which can record and tracks its arguments, return value, the value this and an exception is thrown out of it for all of its calls. So we can check and confirm this information within the spec for any code which is being tested.

We can create two types of spies: as an anonymous function and by wrapping method of an already existing system under the test.

When we don't need to test the behavior of the function under test, we can use the spy as an anonymous function. Here the spy will not do anything else other than recording the information on the call.

We can use spy with wrapping the existing method or function while testing its behavior. In this context, the spy will exactly behave like the original method of function and also gather the information related to the call. So that we can make use of those call details within our spec. Once the test is completed, the spied-on method can be reverted to its original behavior by calling the spy.restore() function.

What is Test Stub?

A test stub is a spy function with pre-programmed behavior. So it behaves like a spy with all of the spy's API available in addition to methods which can be used to modify the stub's behavior.

Just like the spies, the stub can be created as an anonymous function or by wrapping the existing functions. One more difference between the spy and stub is, while using the stub with an existing function wrapped, the original function is not called. So it's our responsibility to add the required behavior to the stub as per the test.

Below are the situations where we can use the stub rather than the spy.

1.   We want to test a particular execution path of the method by controlling its behavior. For testing the error handling, we could force the method to throw an error by stubbing it.

2.   We don't want to call a specific method to avoid an undesired behavior triggered. For testing the database or file system access method, we can stub the method with the expected behavior without actually accessing the database or the file system.

What is Test Mock?

A test mock is a fake method of pre-programmed behavior and pre-programmed expectations. So the mock will behave like a spy and stub along with pre-programmed expectations.

The mock should be used for the method that's being tested in a unit test. Use a mock, if we want to control how the method, which is under test, is being used and like defining the expectations beforehand instead of asserting it later.

You need to install the Sinon package within this application before its use. Run the below command in the terminal from the application's root directory to install and add it as a development dependency in the package.json file.

```
npm install sinon --save-dev
```

2. Load Component Files

Next, let's load the module file which is being tested in this test suite. You can get the service and model attributes from the Cus-tomerModule as below. CustomerService is the unit that you will be testing in this file and CustomerModel is the one that will be mocked.

```
var CustomerModule = require('../../../modules/cus-
tomer/customer.module')();
var CustomerModel = CustomerModule.CustomerModel;
var CustomerService = CustomerModule.CustomerSer-
vice;
```

3. Load Fixtures

Also, fixtures need to be loaded to use as input and write the expec-tation for the unit under test. Below lines will load the fixtures for both the customer and error. Although these fixtures are empty for now, you will be filling them with appropriate content in just a while.

```
var Fixtures = require('../../fixtures/fixtures');
var CustomerFixture = Fixtures.CustomerFixture;
var ErrorFixture = Fixtures.ErrorFixture;
```

Since the CustomerModel will be mocked with Sinon mock API, let's create a variable as well.

```
var CustomerModelMock;
```

4. Prepare Main Test Suite

Next, let's add the below main test suite in the file and more test suites and specs will be inserted inside of this one in the coming sec-tions.

```
describe('CustomerService', function () {
```

```
});
```

Inside this test suite, the specs for testing the createUser function will be added to both success and failure cases. Since you will be running multiple tests for the createCustomer function, let's use the mocking strategy for the CustomerModel when you use it inside the spec. This way you can control the execution of both success and failure paths to simulate the all possible flows of the code.

You should create the mock before the test and destroy it after the test. This preconditions setup and cleanup can be accomplished with the hooks that Mocha provides before(), after(), beforeEach(), and afterEach(). For these tests, the mock needs to be created and destroyed for each test. So you can use the beforeEach() and afterEach() hooks.

So, add the below code blocks inside the main test suite Customer-Service as this will be used for all other test suites that you will be adding in the coming sections as well.

```
beforeEach(function () {
    CustomerModelMock = sinon.mock(CustomerModel);
});
```

The function passed to the beforeEach() will be executed before each test runs. So each time, new CustomerModeMock is created with the use of the Sinon mock API. It mocks the CustomerModel which is used to create and read the Customer document in the MongoDB collection.

```
afterEach(function () {
    CustomerModelMock.restore();

    mongoose.models = {};
    mongoose.modelSchemas = {};
```

```
    return mongoose.connection.close();
});
```

Once a test's execution is completed, the function in the afterEach() will be called. Thus, the mocked CustomerModel function will be restored so that all the behaviors of the actual CustomerModel will be back to its original format and it will be ready for the next test run. The restore() function in the mock is invoked to make it happen.

Also, the next two statements will clear the mongoose models and schemas that are compiled or created during the test run. Finally, the MongoDB connection established via the mongoose module is closed.

7.2.2. Unit Test 11: CreateCustomer Success Test Case

Let's start with the first test suite for the customer.service.js file.

Test Suite

Add a new test suite inside the main suite of the customer.service.spec.js file.

```
describe('createCustomer', function () {

});
```

You would need few variables inside this test suite for holding the fixtures of the customer input to the createCustomer function, expected customer output from the same function and also for the error data. Below are these variables declaration added within the above test suite.

```
var newCustomer, expectedCreatedCustomer, expected-
Error;
```

Test Fixture

As you know already, these fixtures are empty, and they need to be filled in with the appropriate content. Based on the customer details' fields as described in the requirements section, below is the sample content for the new-customer.json fixture file and it is assigned to the newCustomer variable. These attributes value could be different though, as you wish.

```
{
  "firstName": "John",
  "lastName": "Smith",
  "email": "john.smith@example.com",
  "phoneNumber": "9876543210",
  "address": "100 E Street",
  "city": "New York",
  "state": "NY",
  "zipCode": "10000",
  "country": "USA"
}
```

Since MongoDB adds a new attribute '_id' which is of 12 bytes ObjectId format to the customer document as the primary key when it's created, the expectedCreatedCustomer needs to have the same attributes as the input, newCustomer, along with the additional _id attribute. So below will be the content for the created-customer.json. Here the '__v' is also another MongoDB generated attribute for document's version.

```
{
```

```
"_id": "5a5ea8fde43c771e4aa5ea06",
"firstName": "John",
"lastName": "Smith",
"email": "john.smith@example.com",
"phoneNumber": 9876543210,
"address": "100 E Street",
"city": "New York",
"state": "NY",
"zipCode": "10000",
"country": "USA",
"__v": 0
}
```

Test Script

The first spec for the createCustomer would be added next. Here is the spec for the successful path for the createCustomer method call.

```
it('should successfully create new customer', func-
tion () {

});
```

Let's fill in the content in this spec now. First, start with obtaining the test data for the new customer and expected customer result variables from the fixtures.

```
newCustomer = CustomerFixture.newCustomer;
expectedCreatedCustomer = CustomerFixture.created-
Customer;
```

In this test, you will be testing the successful creation of the new customer. To do this test, you will use the CustomerModelMock that was created above. In this mock, you need to define the behavior of the function that will be used to create the customer document in the collection.

The mongoose's Model constructor has create() function, which requires the new customer object as per the CustomerSchema definition as input and returns a promise. Once the customer document is created successfully it will return the newly created document to the caller which can be processed by the function that's passed to the Promise's then function.

Here is the expectation of the successful creation of the customer document with the mock CustomerModelMock. The expectation is defined such a way that, mock has a method called 'create' with the customer object as a parameter and then it returns a promise function with created customer document once the promise is resolved.

```
CustomerModelMock.expects('create')
    .withArgs(newCustomer)
    .resolves(expectedCreatedCustomer);
```

Now comes the central piece of code for this test. As per the low-level design and sequence diagram, CustomerService has to have a method called createCustomer which in turn calls the CustomerModel's create() function to create the new customer in the collection. You already defined the CustomerModel's mock object, CustomerModelMock, with a method and it's parameter and the return value.

So, let's invoke the createCustomer method of the CustomerService and verify all the expectations on the mock with the below code block.

```
return CustomerService.createCustomer(newCustomer)
    .then(function (data) {
        CustomerModelMock.verify();
        expect(data).to.deep.equal(expectedCreated-
Customer);
```

```
});
```

Since this spec is for testing the successful path, let's make use of the promise's 'then' function call. Inside this function, you will be verifying the mock's expectations with the 'CustomerModelMock.verify()' call. Also, the created customer document, which is returned from the createCustomer call, is confirmed to be equivalent to the expected-CreatedCustomer value.

Running this test suite now will show the new spec is failing as we haven't written the functional code for createCustomer yet.

```
1) CustomerService
     createCustomer
       should successfully create new customer:
     TypeError: CustomerService.createCustomer is not a function
       at Context.<anonymous> (tests/unit/customer/customer.service.spec.js:45:36)
```

Code

Let's solve the above error by adding an empty function and expose it via the createCustomer attribute for the module.exports object to the customer.service.js as shown below.

```
(function () {
    'use strict';

    module.exports = {
        createCustomer: createCustomer
    };

    function createCustomer(customer) {

    }
```

```
}) ();
```

After adding this code block, the initial error would have gone away. However, a new exception will be thrown out as below.

```
1) CustomerService
     createCustomer
       should successfully create new customer:
     TypeError: Cannot read property 'then' of undefined
       at Context.<anonymous> (tests/unit/customer/customer.service.spec.js:46:17)
```

This error is because of the createFunction did not return a promise as per the spec's expectation. Invoking the CustomerModel.create() method and returning it will resolve this issue.

At first get the CustomerModel from the CustomerModule file by requiring it. Just below the module.exports object assignment.

```
var CustomerModel = require('./customer.module')
().CustomerModel;
```

Then add the below statement inside the createCustomer function. This function will call the create method of the CustomerModel and returns the promise which comes from the latter method.

```
function createCustomer(customer) {
    return CustomerModel.create(customer);
}
```

With this change, the functional code for creating new customer's successful path of execution is completed as will be shown in the latest test run's successful result.

```
CustomerService
  createCustomer
    ✓   should successfully create new customer
```

7.2.3. Unit Test 12: CreateCustomer Failure Test Case

This spec is to test the failure path of the createCustomer function. Here the expectation would be that the function mentioned earlier will throw an exception while creating the new customer.

Test Fixture

At this juncture, we still the have the empty content for the error-unknown.json file, which we are trying to throw for this spec. Let's complete this file content before we continue with the final step of this test spec. We can assume that there will be some error/exception thrown out of the createCustomer. So, the error could be in any format. To emulate this behavior, without any need to worry about the exception's data structure, we could define that this createFunction throws an unknown error with the below content for the testing purpose.

```
{
  "error": "Unknown",
  "message": "Unknown Error"
}
```

Test Script

You could write the spec for testing the create customer failure as below. Just like the spec for success path, you can start with assigning the test data fixtures for both the input and expected output. Here, the expected output will be an error/exception as we are testing the flow where the create customer function is expected to fail with an exception thrown.

```
it ('should throw error while creating customer',
function () {
    expectedError = ErrorFixture.unknownError;
    newCustomer = CustomerFixture.newCustomer;

    CustomerModelMock.expects ('create')
        .withArgs (newCustomer)
        .rejects (expectedError);

    return CustomerService.createCustomer (newCus-
tomer)
        .catch (function (error) {
            CustomerModelMock.verify ();
            expect (error) .to.deep.equal (expectedEr-
ror);
        });
});
```

The next step would be to set up the behavior and expectation of the function being tested. As you can see in the above code block, we are mocking the 'create' function of the CustomerModelMock with new-Customer as the input for the mocked function and finally making it to reject with an error. It will mock the promise's behavior of throwing an exception.

At the final step, we are invoking the CustomerService's create-Function method with appropriate input, the new customer test fixture, and handling the thrown exception from the CustomerModel-

Mock's create method with the 'catch' block's anonymous function. This block contains the code to verify all the expectations are correct or not. Also, also, the thrown error is checked against the expectedError object to complete the spec.

If we run the mocha test runner now, it will show that all the specs are running successfully, without any more code changes to this spec. That's because the functional code for both success and failure paths are already completed as the CustomerModel's create function is returning a promise. So the failed test case is also passing with same returned promise with the catch function of the promise.

```
CustomerService
  createCustomer
    ✓ should successfully create new customer
    ✓ should throw error while creating customer
```

7.3. CustomerMiddleware - Add Customer Unit Tests

IN THIS SECTION, we will start with writing test scripts and coding the required functional script for the CustomerMiddleware module file for Add Customer functionality.

7.3.1. CustomerMiddleware Spec File Preparation

Let's set up the test file for the customer.middleware.js file now. As per the low-level design for the Add Customer functionality, the middleware function addCustomer will be calling the service function createCustomer with the customer object as input. Then the calling function handles the promise returned from the called function.

1. Load Required Test Modules

We need to prepare the spec file to add the test suites for the testing the behavior mentioned above. Just like previous test files, let's start with the initial test modules loading.

```
'use strict';

var chai = require('chai');
```

```
var expect = chai.expect;
var sinon = require('sinon');
```

Since the middleware function will be dealing with the HTTP request and response objects, we will have to mock these objects as they are external dependencies to the middleware functions. There is a module called 'node-mocks-http' which can be used for mocking these HTTP objects for testing the router or middleware functions. Install this module before we use it by running the below statement on the command line, and this package will be added as a development dependency.

```
npm install node-mocks-http --save-dev
```

Once the package has been downloaded, add the below line in the customer.middleware.spec.js file. This statement will load the node-mocks-http module to the httpMocks variable which will be used to create mockups for the request and response objects in the upcoming specs.

```
var httpMocks = require('node-mocks-http');
```

As the create() function of the CustomerService is also returning a promise, which came from the CustomerModel's create function, we need to either mock or stub the promise for testing the CustomerMiddleware's addCustomer function. We will be using the stubbing approach in this test file. So we need to load the promise module from the bluebird package to use it in the specs.

```
var bluebird = require('bluebird');
var Promise = bluebird.Promise;
```

2. Load Component Files

Next variables to load are the javascript file under test and the other javascript files which are dependencies of the file being tested. Here we are going to test the CustomerMiddleware and CustomerService is the dependency of the former module. Both the modules are loaded via the customer.module.js file as below.

```
var CustomerModule = require('../../../modules/cus-
tomer/customer.module')();
var CustomerMiddleware = CustomerModule.Customer-
Middleware;
var CustomerService = CustomerModule.CustomerSer-
vice;
```

3. Load Fixtures

Let's load the fixtures that are needed for testing both successful and failure paths of the addFunction method. The customer and error fixtures are loaded from the fixtures.js file as below.

```
var Fixtures = require('../../fixtures/fixtures');
var CustomerFixture = Fixtures.CustomerFixture;
var ErrorFixture = Fixtures.ErrorFixture;
```

Finally, let's create the global variables for request and response objects and the next function as well.

```
var req, res, next;
```

4. Prepare Main Test Suite

Now, let's create the main test suite and add the fixtures setup needed before any test spec runs. As this test suites will require request and response objects and next function, we need to create the mocks for these dependencies before each test spec runs. Below code block will take care of this mockup setup activity.

```
describe('CustomerMiddleware', function () {

    beforeEach(function () {
        req = httpMocks.createRequest();
        res = httpMocks.createResponse();
        next = sinon.spy();
    });

});
```

We are using the node-mocks-http module to create the mocks for both HTTP request and response objects. For testing the middleware function's behavior, invoking the next() function in the stack to pass the execution control to, we can create a spy as the next function. This spy function can be used to verify that it was successfully called after adding the customer to the backend database through the service method.

7.3.2. Unit Test 13: AddCustomer Success Test Case

This test is to verify the successful addition of new customer in the MongoDB collection via the middleware function.

Test Suite

Let's create the new test suite for addCustomer function with few required variables declaration as below.

```
describe('addCustomer', function () {
    var createCustomer, createCustomerPromise, ex-
pectedCreatedCustomer, expectedError;

    beforeEach(function () {
        createCustomer = sinon.stub(CustomerSer-
vice, 'createCustomer');
        req.body = CustomerFixture.newCustomer;
    });

    afterEach(function () {
        createCustomer.restore();
    });

});
```

Just like the previous test suites, we need to set up the fixtures before the test spec is written. The beforeEach() and afterEach(), mentioned as above, are performing those tasks. As we discussed earlier, we are creating a stub method, createCustomer, for the CustomerService and also the newCustomer fixtures is assigned to the request's body object as it will be parsed inside the middleware function to pass it onto the service to create the customer.

Test Script

Next, we will create the spec for testing the addCustomer method of the CustomerMiddleware. Inside this spec, at first, expected output and the expected behavior of the dependent function createCustomer is defined. So when we invoke the addCustomer function, which is under test, the stubbed function will behave as it's defined in the spec with the expected input and output.

```
it('should successfully create new customer', func-
tion () {
    expectedCreatedCustomer = CustomerFixture.cre-
atedCustomer;

    createCustomerPromise = Promise.resolve(expect-
edCreatedCustomer);
    createCustomer.withArgs(req.body).returns(cre-
ateCustomerPromise);

    CustomerMiddleware.addCustomer(req, res, next);

    sinon.assert.callCount(createCustomer, 1);

    return createCustomerPromise.then(function () {
        expect(req.response).to.be.a('object');
        expect(req.response).to.deep.equal(expect-
edCreatedCustomer);
        sinon.assert.callCount(next, 1);
    });

});
```

Let's break this code block line by line and see what each of those lines does. Here, at the first line of it() block, we are assigning the variable expectedCreatedCustomer with the fixture data.

```
expectedCreatedCustomer = CustomerFixture.created-
Customer;
```

The statement is defining a behavior of the Promise function to resolve with the expected output when it's successfully complemented the operation.

```
createCustomerPromise = Promise.resolve(expected-
```

```
CreatedCustomer);
```

At the third line, we are defining the behavior of the dependent method, which should be called from inside the CustomerMiddleware's addFunction method. The stubbed function is called with the request's body object as input and returns the successful promise function with the expected output data, the expectedCreatedCustomer.

```
createCustomer.withArgs(req.body).returns(create-
CustomerPromise);
```

So far, the behavior and expectation of the spec are set up, and the next statement is invoking the function under test to verify it's behavior.

```
CustomerMiddleware.addCustomer(req, res, next);
```

The rest of the statements in it() block are verifying or asserting the addCustomer's behavior as expected or defined already. The below line asserts that the createCustomer() function is invoked once.

```
sinon.assert.callCount(createCustomer, 1);
```

Last code block asserts that the middleware function under test is handling the promise function returned by the stubbed service function. Also, the output returned by the successful promise function is checked against the expected output. A response attribute is an object, which is supposed to be set in the request object by the middleware function and is of same structure and content as the expectedCreatedCustomer.

```
return createCustomerPromise.then(function () {
    expect(req.response).to.be.a('object');
    expect(req.response).to.deep.equal(expectedCre-
atedCustomer);
    sinon.assert.callCount(next, 1);
});
```

Finally, the next() function invocation is also verified with sinon's assert API. As usual, when we run the test suites once again will show one failing spec as shown below.

```
1) CustomerMiddleware
     addCustomer
       should successfully create new customer:
     TypeError: CustomerMiddleware.addCustomer is not a function
      at Context.<anonymous> (tests/unit/customer/customer.middleware.spec.js:46:32)
```

Code

As the next logical step, we will have to write the functional code to make the failing test to pass. Let's start with adding an empty function addCustomer in the customer.middleware.js file.

```
(function () {
    'use strict';

    module.exports = {
        addCustomer: addCustomer
    };

    function addCustomer(req, res, next) {}

})();
```

After adding the above code and running the test suites will show that we resolved the above mentioned 'CustomerMiddleware.add-Customer is not a function' error. However, it will also throw the below error as we haven't completed the expected behavior of the add-Customer function yet.

```
1) CustomerMiddleware
    addCustomer
      should successfully create new customer:
   AssertError: expected createCustomer to be called once but was called 0 times
     at Object.fail (node_modules/sinon/lib/sinon/assert.js:96:21)
     at failAssertion (node_modules/sinon/lib/sinon/assert.js:55:16)
     at Object.assertCallCount [as callCount] (node_modules/sinon/lib/sinon/assert.js:137:13)
     at Context.<anonymous> (tests/unit/customer/customer.middleware.spec.js:48:26)
```

As the expected behavior is written in the spec file and if we keep writing the functional code to satisfy the failing behavior, the operational code will be written entirely. So, let's continue with code which will resolve the error mentioned above.

Since the latest error shows that createCustomer method is not called once, we will write the required code make it invoke once inside the addCustomer function. Since we already have the service function created inside the customer.service.js file, let's load the service module inside the middleware through the module file as below just after the module.exports statement.

```
var CustomerService = require('./customer.module')
().CustomerService;
```

If we add the code to invoke the CustomerService.createCustomer() inside the addCustomer function, we will have resolved the current error shown as above.

```
function addCustomer(req, res, next) {
    CustomerService.createCustomer(req.body);
```

}

Now we will face another error as the expectation of req.response is not met yet.

```
1) CustomerMiddleware
      addCustomer
        should successfully create new customer:
      AssertionError: expected undefined to be an object
```

To make this behavior passed and createCustomer is returning the promise function, let's add the promise handling function for successful operation. Inside this successful promise handler function, assign the data returned from the CustomerService.createCustomer() function to the req.response attribute. Here is the updated addCustomer function with the latest changes.

```
function addCustomer(req, res, next) {

    CustomerService.createCustomer(req.body)
        .then(success);

    function success(data) {
        req.response = data;
    }

}
```

We will notice that one more expectation is satisfied and the 'undefined' error would have gone. Now, comes the next and final error for this test spec.

```
1) CustomerMiddleware
     addCustomer
       should successfully create new customer:
     AssertError: expected spy to be called once but was called 0 times
```

This expectation is for the next() function to be called once inside the success handler function of the createCustomer()'s promise. Just by adding the 'next()' statement after the req.response attribute assignment, all the expectations of the addCustomer spec would be met, and we will see no more errors at this time. This addition will also make sure that this addCustomer middleware function passes the execution control to the next available middleware function in the stack as per the definition of the middleware function.

Here is the completed middleware file content for the test suites that we had written so far.

```
(function () {
    'use strict';

    module.exports = {
        addCustomer: addCustomer
    };

    var CustomerService = require('./customer.mod-
ule')().CustomerService;

    function addCustomer(req, res, next) {

        CustomerService.createCustomer(req.body)
            .then(success);

        function success(data) {
            req.response = data;
```

```
        next();
      }

   }

})();
```

So here is the successful test suite's result for the addCustomer functionality so far.

```
CustomerMiddleware
  addCustomer
    ✓  should successfully create new customer
```

7.3.3. Unit Test 14: AddCustomer Failure Test Case

So far, we have completed the test suite and functional code for the execution path of successful customer addition for the middleware function. We also need to test the negative test case.

Test Script

Here is the complete test spec for the failure execution path for customer creation function of the CustomerMiddleware. Assume there is an error occurred while creating the customer and we want to make sure that error has been appropriately handled without crashing the application. This spec will test that error handling part of the create-Customer function.

```
it('should throw error while creating the new cus-
```

```
tomer', function () {
    expectedError = ErrorFixture.unknownError;

    createCustomerPromise = Promise.reject(expect-
edError);
    createCustomer.withArgs(req.body).returns(cre-
ateCustomerPromise);

    CustomerMiddleware.addCustomer(req, res, next);

    sinon.assert.callCount(createCustomer, 1);

    return createCustomerPromise.catch(function
(error) {
        expect(error).to.be.a('object');
        expect(error).to.deep.equal(expectedError);
    });

});
```

To begin with the new spec for testing the error while creating the customer, below it() block is needed.

```
it('should throw error while creating the new cus-
tomer', function () {

});
```

Next, the local variables for expectedError and createdCustomer-Promise are assigned with the appropriate initial values and behavior. We can assign the unknownError from the error fixture for the expectedError. Also, the Promise's rejected behavior is assigned to the createdCustomerPromise variable.

Once the required data fixtures have been set up, let's make the createCustomer() function call with all the inputs as below.

```
CustomerMiddleware.addCustomer(req, res, next);
```

Next two statements are for confirming the expected behavior of the error execution path. First, we are making sure that the service function createCustomer is called from within the middleware's addCustomer function. Finally, we are testing the error handler function for the promise returned from the CustomerService's createCustomer function. In this catch block, the thrown error is expected to be equal to the unknownError object.

```
sinon.assert.callCount(createCustomer, 1);

    return createCustomerPromise.catch(function
(error) {
        expect(error).to.be.a('object');
        expect(error).to.deep.equal(expectedError);
    });
```

After this, if we run the test, we will get the below error. It is because there is no code which satisfies the test case that we just wrote.

```
CustomerMiddleware
  addCustomer
    ✓  should successfully create new customer
    ✓  should throw error while creating the new customer
Unhandled rejection (<{"error":"Unknown","message":"Unknown ...>, no stack trace)
```

Code

We can quickly fix the above error just by adding the catch

block to capture and handle the promise error thrown from service call inside the middleware's addCustomer function. Below is the modified function with added catch block which invokes the failure() function to handle the error thrown.

```
function addCustomer(req, res, next) {

    CustomerService.createCustomer(req.body)
        .then(success)
        .catch(failure);

    function success(data) {
        req.response = data;
        next();
    }

    function failure(error) {
        next(error);
    }

}
```

So finally, we have all the test suites passed for the middleware function addCustomer, both success and failure execution paths.

```
CustomerMiddleware
  addCustomer
    ✓  should successfully create new customer
    ✓  should throw error while creating the new customer
```

7.4. CustomerController - Add Customer API Integration Test

WE HAVE COMPLETED the unit tests for both middleware and service so far. How about testing the controller functions? Since the controller contains the route definitions and handler functions for the API endpoints, the test we could run is called an integration test, which mainly tests the end to end functionality of the API endpoint. The integration test can be used to test the module's single functionality with all the layers underneath grouped.

So, testing the controller's route definition will execute the middleware function calls, and in turn, service function calls till the last layer in the stack of the API endpoint. Here we cannot mock or stub any of the dependencies for any of the functions in the execution flow. Thus, we will end up creating the actual customer document in the MongoDB collection when we run the integration test for the add customer API endpoint definition.

In this section, we will go over the steps to create the integration test suites for the Add Customer functionality for both successful customer creation and failed customer creation execution paths.

7.4.1. CustomerController Spec File Preparation

Just like the unit test spec file, we will start with setting up the integration test spec file as well. Since we will be testing only the controller file per module, to test all the functionality of that particular module, we may not need to create directory 'customer' under the /tests/integration to create the integration test suite files for the customer module.

If we add more than one controller file to this module for some reason, later on, we could refactor the directory structure with module specific directory for all it's controller spec files grouped them.

1. Load Required Test Modules

For now, let's create the customer.controller.spec.js file under the /tests/integration directory with below initial content.

```
'use strict';

var chai = require('chai');
var chaiHttp = require('chai-http');
chai.use(chaiHttp);

var expect = chai.expect;
var request = chai.request;
```

These are lines usual test file contents except one new module, 'chai-http'. As the controller file will contain the routing definitions for the API endpoints to handle all the incoming requests specific to the customer module, we have to test the request and response related functionalities at this file. To test these HTTP request and response, we would need a testing library which supports HTTP testing.

Chai has several plugins to support various unit and integration testing needs of a developer. One of the integration plugins for HTTP is, chai-http. This Chai assertion library's plugin supports testing HTTP apps or external services by integration testing with request composition and response assertions. As usual, this plugin can be installed within the express application with below command, which will add it as a development dependency for the customer-service application.

```
npm install chai-http —save-dev
```

2. Load Fixtures

Once the required modules are loaded for integration testing, we need to load the file under test and fixtures for the testing. This task is accomplished with below lines.

```
var app = require('../../app');

var Fixtures = require('../fixtures/fixtures');
var CustomerFixture = Fixtures.CustomerFixture;
```

Here, we are creating a variable 'app' and loaded with the whole express application itself, by requiring the app.js file from the root directory. So then, loading the customer fixture from the fixtures file.

We need to know the base URI for the Customer API endpoints so that we could form the complete URI for testing and developing the individual API endpoint's functionalities. Here is the base URI we could start with.

```
var baseUri = '/customers';
```

3. Prepare Main Test Suite

Finally, we will create the main test suites for the controller file as below. All the test specs will be added within this main describe()

block as we go ahead with creating the integration test cases for all the endpoints of this module.

```
describe('CustomerController', function () {

});
```

7.4.2. Integration Test 1: Add Customer API

Let's begin the integration test suite for creating new customer API with the empty describe block, where we will continue with the spec further.

Test Suite

As you know already, from the sequence diagram of low-level design, to create a new customer, we will use the POST HTTP method for the API endpoint. This HTTP method will be associated with the endpoint URI '/customers', which tells the express application that we want to add a new customer to the system.

```
describe("POST " + baseUri, function () {

});
```

Test Script

Inside this test suite, the test spec for calling the add customer API endpoint will be added. Below is the initial code with it() block for this spec.

```
it('should add new customer', function (done) {
```

```
});
```

The parameter 'done' in this spec is added to be passed as a callback to the HTTP request so that once the asynchronous request is completed, it will be invoked. This invocation of the callback will indicate that the HTTP call to the API endpoint is completed and then spec's execution will be finished.

This capability is provided by Mocha framework to enable the developers to write unit/integration tests for any asynchronous code, APIs or external systems.

Now, we will write the code to test the behavior of the add customer API. Below is completed test script for this spec. Let's go through each component of this code block one by one.

```
describe("POST " + baseUri, function () {
    it('should add new customer', function (done) {

        request(app)
            .post(baseUri)
            .send(CustomerFixture.newCustomer)
            .end(function (err, res) {

                expect(res.status).to.equal(201);
                expect(res.body).to.not.equal({});
                expect(res.body._id).to.not.equal(un-
defined);
expect(res.body.firstName).to.equal(CustomerFix-
ture.createdCustomer.firstName);

                done();

            });

    });

});
```

```
});
```

In this spec, we are using the chai's HTTP plugin for composing the request and handling the response object of API endpoint. The below piece of code represents the request composition and invokes the POST HTTP request to the baseUri, /customers, with the newCustomer fixture content as the request body.

```
request(app)
    .post(baseUri)
    .send(CustomerFixture.newCustomer)
    .end(function (err, res) {

        done();
    });
```

As this is an asynchronous call, the end() block waits until the request is completed and invokes the anonymous function inside to continue with the testing to verify the expected behavior of the API. We will see how the expected behavior is confirmed in just a while. Once the verification is completed the callback function done() is invoked to let the Mocha test runner know that the test is finished and it's execution can be ended at this moment.

Let's continue with rest of the piece of code within the end() block now. As the asynchronous request returns either successful data or the error thrown from the API call, we are getting both the error and response objects in this block.

As this test is an integration test and we cannot mock or stub any dependencies and alter the behavior or the response of the code under test, we can add the expected behavior verification scripts. If all the behavior is as per our scripted expectation in this code block, we can assume that the API endpoint is working as expected otherwise there is an integration issue, and we need to look into it to fix it.

```
expect(res.status).to.equal(200);
expect(res.body).to.not.equal({});
expect(res.body._id).to.not.equal(undefined);
expect(res.body.firstName
).to.equal(CustomerFixture.createdCustomer.first-
Name
);
```

The first expectation would be that HTTP status code from the response should be successful with 200 and rest of the expectations are based on the expected createdCustomer fixture as the response body should be same as the expected data that we provided. Here we are testing for certain parts of the response object to make sure that it meets the test spec's expectation. With this script, we can conclude this spec definition.

If we run the test now, we should be getting the error as shown below. We will continue with functional code development to fix the errors one by one in the next section.

```
1) CustomerController
     POST /customers
       should add new customer:

     Uncaught AssertionError: expected 404 to equal 201
     + expected - actual

     -404
     +201
```

Code

It's time to start adding the required code in the controller file for exposing the API endpoint and adding the API URI's handling functions. As you know the CustomerController is loading the router object as the module, we will have to add the add customer endpoint URI '/customers' into the router's post method along with middleware functions added as handler methods for the add customer path URI.

We can begin by creating the variable for loading the Customer-Middleware module right after the already existing variables for express and router modules assignment in the customer.controller.js file as below.

```
var CustomerMiddleware = require('./customer.module')().CustomerMiddleware;
```

Let's add the below code block after the middleware variable and just before the router object's assignment to the module.exports object. What we are doing in these statements are, any request to the '/customer/' path with post HTTP method will be handled by this route definition.

```
router.post('/',
    function (req, res) {
        res.status(201).json({});
    });
```

Even though we added the above route definition in the controller file, running the test suites will still yield the same error messages as there is nothing defined in the app.js which says that CustomerController will be handling any request with '/customers' base URI path. So we need to add some code to the apps.js to do so.

As mentioned in the controller's spec file, the whole express application is loaded via the app.js from which we are making the HTTP post request to the base URI '/customers'. Even though there is the CustomerController file available in the module, we have not explicitly defined that this controller file will be handling all the requests to the '/customers' base URI in this RESTful service. So let's instruct the app to do so with below statements.

As usual, we can get the CustomerController module from the customer.module.js file and assign it to the variable with the same name. Let's add this line just below the MongoDBUtil variable in the app.js file.

```
var CustomerController = require('./modules/customer/customer.module')().CustomerController;
```

Then, we can add the below line just after the MongoDB connection initialization statement.

```
app.use('/customers', CustomerController);
```

The above statement tells the express application to pass any request with the base URI '/customers' path to the CustomerController router object.

Now, if we ran the Mocha test, we have passed the previous error for the status code but faced with new error as below as the next expectation is failing. Let's continue to fix one by one until we see no more failing spec's expectation.

```
1) CustomerController
     POST /customers
       should add new customer:
     Uncaught AssertionError: expected undefined to not equal undefined
```

The last piece that could get the latest error fixed is available in the middleware. We need to plug in the addCustomer middleware function of the CustomerMiddleware in this route definition. This function will create the new customer in the MongoDB collection through the service and set the newly created customer document in the response attribute in the request. Below is the completed code block for the test spec that we just wrote.

```
router.post('/',
    CustomerMiddleware.addCustomer,
    function (req, res) {
        res.status(201).json(req.response);
    });
```

As we have added the functional code to satisfy all the expectations of the test suite, the test should pass without any error now. Below is the screenshot of the passing test suite of the controller file so far.

```
CustomerController
    POST /customers
POST /customers 201 11.380 ms - 228
    ✓  should add new customer
```

With this integration test, we have completed the development of Add Customer API with Test-Driven Development approach.

Step 05 - Add Customer API - GitHub

YOU CAN FIND the code that we completed so far in the below Git-Hub repository. Please feel free to check out the whole codebase and explore this step's files in the **Step 05 - Add Customer API** directory.

GitHub Repository:

https://github.com/parripandian/building-nodejs-api-with-tdd-approach

Current Step Directory:

https://github.com/parripandian/building-nodejs-api-with-tdd-approach/tree/master/Step%2005%20-%20Add%20Customer%20API

Chapter 8: *Get Customer List API*

8.1. Get Customer List Functionality

ONCE WE ADDED the customer data in the backend database, we should be able to query the available customers whenever needed. So, as described in the Low-level design of the Get Customers List functionality, the GET HTTP method will be used to call the API endpoint '/customers' with any search, filter and pagination parameters.

In this chapter, we will go through the unit and integration tests scripts and functional coding without any additional functionalities such as search, filter and pagination.

8.2. CustomerService - Fetch Customers Unit Tests

IN THIS SECTION, we will start with writing test scripts and coding the required functional script for the CustomerService module file for Get Customer List functionality.

8.2.1. Unit Test 15: FetchCustomers Success Test Case

We will start by adding test scripts for the customer.service.js file.

Test Suite

To add the test suite for testing the fetchCustomers method in service file, we will create the describe() block in the customer.service.spec.js file under the /tests/unit/customer directory.

As already we have the createCustomer test suite in this file, so, let's add the below code block just below the existing test suite inside the main describe() block of the CustomerService.

```
describe('fetchCustomers', function () {
                var expectedCustomers, expect-
edError;
});
```

The declared local variables expectedCustomers and expectedError are for setting up the expected data for testing the response from the service call once it's completed.

Test Fixture

If you look at the fixture file /tests/fixtures/customer/customers.json, you will notice that it's still empty. So, we need to update this file with a list of customers test data for this specific spec. Just fill up this file with the below content, to begin with.

```
[
  {
    "_id": "5a5ea8fde43c771e4aa5ea06",
    "firstName": "John",
    "lastName": "Smith",
    "email": "john.smith@example.com",
    "phoneNumber": 9876543210,
    "address": "100 E Street",
    "city": "New York",
    "state": "NY",
    "zipCode": "10000",
    "country": "USA",
    "__v": 0
  },
  {
    "_id": "5a5ea8fde43c771e4aa5ea07",
    "firstName": "Jane",
    "lastName": "Smith",
    "email": "jane.smith@example.com",
    "phoneNumber": 9876522222,
    "address": "100 E Street",
    "city": "New York",
    "state": "NY",
```

```
    "zipCode":  "10000",
    "country":  "USA",
    "__v":  0
  }
]
```

Test Script

As the first spec for the fetchCustomers method, we can start writing the test scripts for the successful flow of fetching all the customers that are already created in the MongoDB collection via the createCustomer method. This requires the below it() block with necessary details setup initially before any expected behavior of this function is scripted.

```
it('should successfully fetch all customers', func-
tion () {

});
```

As with any unit test cases, this one should also follow the same steps for testing the fetchCustomers() method of the CustomerService module. The three steps are as follows:

1. Setting up the expected response of the method under test.
2. Mocking or stubbing the behavior of the dependencies of the method under test.
3. Invoking the method that is being tested and confirming the expected behavior by verifying the response against the expected response.

Let's start with setting up the expectedCustomers variable by fetching customers data from the CustomerFixture as below.

```
expectedCustomers = CustomerFixture.customers;
```

Next, we have to set up the dependency of the fetchCustomers() function. As with the createCustomer() function, the same CustomerModel is the dependency for this method also. There is already a mock object CustomerModelMock created for this model object; we could continue to set up the behavior for fetching the customers from the customers collection. Here is the completed code for this step.

```
CustomerModelMock.expects('find')
    .withArgs({})
    .chain('exec')
    .resolves(expectedCustomers);
```

What we are doing here is, adding a method called 'find' to the CustomerModelMock with the empty object '{}' as an argument. Then, adding another 'exec' by chaining it to the previously added method. Finally, setting this behavior to resolve a promise with the expectedCustomers fixture data as the response for the promise. If you notice that we added a new term 'chain' to the mock behavior to chain the multiple methods. It is new from the mock that we set up so far.

We are using two of the Mongoose model's methods find and exec here. The find method returns the query object with empty object {} as the query parameter, which means when this query is executed later it will return all the documents from the customers collection. The next method 'exec' is to execute the previously formed query object through the 'find' method call. This second method will execute the query and returns the result. Also, you might have observed that this method was set to return a promise when it gets executed. That's because the 'exec' method will return a promise when there is no callback method is passed to it. This how we expect our fetchCustomers() function to behave when we implement the functional logic later on.

To use the .chain() method, we need to import a new module 'sinon-mongoose' which extends the Sinon stubs for Mongoose methods to test any chained methods. So let's import this new module to the package.json as a development dependency by running the below statement in the command line.

```
npm install sinon-mongoose --save-dev
```

Also, add the requiring the module within this spec file just below sinon variable declarations. So updated lines will look as below.

```
var sinon = require('sinon');
require('sinon-mongoose');
```

As the last step, we need to invoke the fetchCustomers() method of the CustomerService and verify the Mock object's expectation as defined. Also, we can further check to confirm that the method under test returns the expected output as defined in the expectation as well. Let's look at the below-completed code for the final step.

```
return CustomerService.fetchCustomers()
    .then(function (data) {
        CustomerModelMock.verify();
        expect(data).to.deep.equal(expectedCus-
tomers);
    });
```

Here, we are invoking the fetchCustomers() method, as we are testing the successful execution path, we have the then() block to handle the promise's returned data. Inside this block, we are verifying the mocked model's behavior just by calling the verify() function of the CustomerModelMock object and also confirming the returned data from by the promise is same as the expectedCustomers data. It will make sure the expected behavior of the fetchCustomers() method is as we defined.

As usual, below will be the error message when running the mocha test now.

```
1) CustomerService
      fetchCustomers
        should successfully fetch all customers:
     TypeError: CustomerService.fetchCustomers is not a function
      at Context.<anonymous> (tests/unit/customer/customer.service.spec.js:81:36)
```

Code

So, now we got the error message which mentions there is no function called fetchCustomers() in the CustomerService, lets starting writing the functional code for fetchCustomers() method by adding to the customer.service.file.

To solve the above issue, let's add the new function fetchCustomers() with empty content and add it to the module.exports() object as below.

```
module.exports = {
    createCustomer: createCustomer,
    fetchCustomers: fetchCustomers
};
```

Also, the empty function.

```
function fetchCustomers() {
}
```

This would have fixed the error mentioned above but yet yielded the new error message as below.

```
1) CustomerService
     fetchCustomers
        should successfully fetch all customers:
      TypeError: Cannot read property 'then' of undefined
      at Context.<anonymous> (tests/unit/customer/customer.service.spec.js:82:17)
```

The new error shows that fetchCustomers() method should return a promise so that test spec can invoke this method and handle the successful response with the then() function.

So, let's add the required code to query all the documents and execute the query and then return the promise of the query execution. Below is the completed code for this function.

```
function fetchCustomers() {
    return CustomerModel.find({})
        .exec();
}
```

By completing the fetchCustomers() function with the required code will show that spec's expectation is met and we finished the unit test for the successful execution path for the method under test. You will see the test results as below when you rerun the test.

```
CustomerService
  createCustomer
    ✓ should successfully create new customer
    ✓ should throw error while creating customer
  fetchCustomers
    ✓ should successfully fetch all customers
```

8.2.2. Unit Test 16: FetchCustomers Failure Test Case

In this section, we will write the spec for the negative test case for fetchCustomers() method of the CustomerService to make sure that failure execution path also handled properly by the functional code.

Test Script

To test the failed execution path for the method under test will require all the same steps as the successful spec except few things like it will expect an error thrown by the invoked method and the error will be handled by the catch() method of the promise object which was thrown by the mocked model object.

Here is the completed spec for this test case. It () block describes that this spec is for testing the error handling the behavior of the fetchCustomers() method. As a first step, we are setting up the expectedError from the ErrorFixture. Next would be the mocked CustomerModel object's error throwing behavior with all other conditions, like the input and the chaining of the invoked methods of the dependent model object, are same as the previous test for successful execution path. The returned promise will be coming up with the error output for this use case.

```
it('should throw error while fetching all cus-
tomers', function () {
    expectedError = ErrorFixture.unknownError;

    CustomerModelMock.expects('find')
        .withArgs({})
        .chain('exec')
        .rejects(expectedError);
```

```
    return CustomerService.fetchCustomers()
        .catch(function (error) {
            CustomerModelMock.verify();
            expect(error).to.deep.equal(expectedEr-
ror);
        });
});
```

Finally, the confirmation of the behavior for the failure within the fetchCustomers() method. Here, we are comparing the error returned by the CustomerService's method and comparing it to the expected-Error as per the testing fixture data.

Now, you would wonder if this test case shows an error message when the test runner runs next time.

Code

It wouldn't and shouldn't show any more error message in the test results. Because all the functional code written so far will be sufficient for this test script as well. There is no additional functional code needed for testing the failed execution path for the fetchCustomers()'s functionality.

Below is the screenshot of the test results after the latest test spec added.

```
CustomerService
  createCustomer
    ✓ should successfully create new customer
    ✓ should throw error while creating customer
  fetchCustomers
    ✓ should successfully fetch all customers
    ✓ should throw error while fetching all customers
```

8.3. CustomerMiddleware - Get Customers Unit Tests

LET'S CONTINUE WITH the middleware method testing and development in this section. Here, we will have to write the test suite for the CustomerMiddleware's getCustomers() function, as per the low-level design.

8.3.1. Unit Test 17: GetCustomers Success Test Case

For this new unit test case, we will start with setting up the test suite, then test script and finally, the code to satisfy the middleware function's test spec.

Test Suite

There will be a new suite added in the customer.middleware.spec.js file with the describe() block as below to begin with.

```
describe('getCustomers', function () {
});
```

Inside this describe block, we need to add some variables declarations and preconditions setup and cleanup blocks as well. As we are utiliz-

ing the stubbing approach for setting up the dependent CustomerService for the middleware module for the previous test suite 'addCustomer,' we will continue to use the same for this suite. So, below will
be the updated describe() block with changes mentioned above applied.

```
describe('getCustomers', function () {
    var fetchCustomers, fetchCustomersPromise, ex-
pectedCustomers, expectedError;

    beforeEach(function () {
        fetchCustomers = sinon.stub(CustomerSer-
vice, 'fetchCustomers');
        req.body = {};
    });

    afterEach(function () {
        fetchCustomers.restore();
    });

});
```

In the first line, we are declaring the variables for the stubbed method,
and its promise function output. Also, we have the variables for the
output data for the successful execution path testing and error data
for the failed execution path testing.

The next code block, beforeEach(), is creating the stub method
fetchCustomers() for the CustomerService, which is a dependency for
the current method under the test. Also, the cleanup function, after-
Each(), comes, at last, to restore the stubbed method of the service
module once each test execution is finished.

Test Script

To start the first middleware test for the getCustomers() method, let's create it() block for the successful execution path test spec as below with complete script.

```
it('should successfully get all customers', func-
tion () {
    expectedCustomers = CustomerFixture.customers;

    fetchCustomersPromise = Promise.resolve(expect-
edCustomers);
    fetchCustomers.returns(fetchCustomersPromise);

    CustomerMiddleware.getCustomers(req, res,
next);

    sinon.assert.callCount(fetchCustomers, 1);

    return fetchCustomersPromise.then(function () {
        expect(req.response).to.be.a('array');
        expect(req.response.length).to.equal(ex-
pectedCustomers.length);
        expect(req.response).to.deep.equal(expect-
edCustomers);
        sinon.assert.callCount(next, 1);
    });

});
```

In this spec, we are following the same steps as other specs that we have written so far. The expectedCustomers variable can be pre-populated with the test data from CustomerFixture.

Since the middleware method getCustomers() will be receiving a promise from the service method fetchCustomers() when it's called, we are adding the expected behavior to the stubbed method with below lines code. A promise is created using the Promise object of the bluebird module by setting it up to resolve and return the expected-Customers test data when the dependent method call completed.

```
fetchCustomersPromise = Promise.resolve(expected-
Customers);
fetchCustomers.returns(fetchCustomersPromise);
```

Next, we are invoking the method under test, getCustomers() of the CustomerMiddleware, to test its behavior. Right after that, we are asserting that the dependent method, fetchCustomers stub, was called only once.

```
CustomerMiddleware.getCustomers(req, res, next);
sinon.assert.callCount(fetchCustomers, 1);
```

Finally, to confirm and validate the expected behavior of the service method's successful path, the then() block of the returned promise, we have added expectations of the data returned inside the same block. Here, we need to check that the returned data is an array of the customers and it's of the same length and same data structure with values as the test data. The invocation of the next() function can also be confirmed within this assertion block.

```
return fetchCustomersPromise.then(function () {
    expect(req.response).to.be.a('array');
    expect(req.response.length).to.equal(expected-
Customers.length);
    expect(req.response).to.deep.equal(expectedCus-
tomers);
    sinon.assert.callCount(next, 1);
});
```

It completes our spec for the successful execution path of the getCus-
tomers() middleware function. The below would be the test result
when running the test suites at this moment. To solve this issue, we
need to continue with the next section.

```
1) CustomerMiddleware
     getCustomers
       should successfully get all customers:
     TypeError: CustomerMiddleware.getCustomers is not a function
       at Context.<anonymous> (tests/unit/customer/customer.middleware.spec.js:95:32)
```

Code

Whenever we encounter the error which says that a method is not a
function of the module that we are testing against, the first step to do
is creating the named method with empty content and expose it from
the module itself. Just like the below scripts for the customer.middle-
ware.js file. These scripts will be added at the appropriate locations
inside the js file.

```
module.exports = {
    addCustomer: addCustomer,
    getCustomers: getCustomers
};

function getCustomers(req, res, next) {
}
```

As the getCustomers() is a middleware function, it needs the request,
response and next as inputs to comply with its nature. This time when
you run the tests will yield new error as below as the method is not
complete yet.

```
1) CustomerMiddleware
     getCustomers
       should successfully get all customers:
   AssertError: expected fetchCustomers to be called once but was called 0 times
     at Object.fail (node_modules/sinon/lib/sinon/assert.js:96:21)
     at failAssertion (node_modules/sinon/lib/sinon/assert.js:55:16)
     at Object.assertCallCount [as callCount] (node_modules/sinon/lib/sinon/assert.js:137:13)
     at Context.<anonymous> (tests/unit/customer/customer.middleware.spec.js:97:26)
```

For the new error, adding the script to call the service method fetch-Customers() with promise handling method blocks would be required.

In the handler function for the promise's successful response will assign the returned the fetched data to the response attribute in the request which will be used in the controller layer. Then it will have to invoke the next() function to continue with the request-response lifecycle.

Here is the completed getCustomers() method with all the expected behavior is coded.

```
function getCustomers(req, res, next) {

    CustomerService.fetchCustomers()
        .then(success);

    function success(data) {
        req.response = data;
        next();
    }

}
```

As all the required functionality of the method under the test is completed, now we should be getting the successful test run with below results for the CustomerMiddleware's test specs.

```
CustomerMiddleware
  addCustomer
    ✓  should successfully create new customer
    ✓  should throw error while creating the new customer
  getCustomers
    ✓  should successfully get all customers
```

8.3.2. Unit Test 18: GetCustomers Failure Test Case

Now we will go through the failure execution path of the getCustomers() middleware function testing. With this test, all the unit test cases for the get customers list functionality will be completed.

Test Script

Let's add it() block for this purpose stated in its description as below. We need to populate the test data expectedError from the Error-Fixture's unknownError json object. When we set up the behavior for the stubbed function fetchCustomers() of the service module, we need to make sure that its promise is rejecting with the error object.

Next would the same step as the success path, that's calling the getCustomers() function and asserting the one call count of the fetchCustomers() method. Finally, we will be comparing the returned error object from the invoked method with the expectedError variable. All these steps are written as the script as below.

```
it('should throw error while getting all
customers', function () {
    expectedError = ErrorFixture.unknownError;
```

```
    fetchCustomersPromise = Promise.reject(expect-
edError);
    fetchCustomers.returns(fetchCustomersPromise);

    CustomerMiddleware.getCustomers(req,   res,
next);

    sinon.assert.callCount(fetchCustomers, 1);

    return fetchCustomersPromise.catch(function
(error) {
        expect(error).to.be.a('object');
        expect(error).to.deep.equal(expectedError);
    });

});
```

When we run the test suites we should see an error message as below which is because we haven't written the catch() block inside the middleware function to capture the error from the service method call. We will fix this issue in the coming section. Here is the error that we will see now.

```
CustomerMiddleware
  addCustomer
    ✓  should successfully create new customer
    ✓  should throw error while creating the new customer
  getCustomers
    ✓  should successfully get all customers
    ✓  should throw error while getting all customers
Unhandled rejection (<{"error":"Unknown","message":"Unknown ...>, no stack trace)
```

Code

To resolve the unhandled rejection error for the getCustomers()

method call, we need to add the catch() block which will handle the promise's rejected path and set the error object in the next() call itself so that the error will be processed at the application level. If you add the necessary script for this error capturing part the completed code will be looking as shown below.

```
function getCustomers(req, res, next) {

    CustomerService.fetchCustomers()
        .then(success)
        .catch(failure);

    function success(data) {
        req.response = data;
        next();
    }

    function failure(err) {
        next(err);
    }

}
```

Here is the final test result's screenshot the next test run will show after the above code is written.

```
CustomerMiddleware
  addCustomer
    ✓ should successfully create new customer
    ✓ should throw error while creating the new customer
  getCustomers
    ✓ should successfully get all customers
    ✓ should throw error while getting all customers
```

8.4. CustomerController - Get Customer List API Integration Test

NOW, LET'S CONTINUE with the integration test for the Get Customer List functionality. In this section, we will actually test the API endpoint for this functionality which will start with the controller and passes down the request through the middleware and service layers and fetches the data from the MongoDB collection and finally returns the fetched data to the client.

8.4.1. Integration Test 2: Get Customer List API

To run the test for the API endpoint '/customers' with GET HTTP method, we need to start writing the test suite for this controller functionality in the customer.controller.js file

Test Suite

Just below the already written integration test the for the create customer API endpoint, add the below describe() block to add the test suite for the current functionality API. As this is for testing the customer module's base URI with GET HTTP method, add the describe() block with an appropriate description which defines the test case's nature.

```
describe("GET " + baseUri, function () {
});
```

Inside the test suite, it() block for the test spec will have to be added with the required description of the spec along with the callback 'done' passed as an input parameter which will be invoked once the asynchronous call to the GET API is completed with the response.

Test Script

As you see the completed spec script as below, we have to write the HTTP call to the express app with the base URI with the GET HTTP method call for the integration test to simulate the actual API calling process. Within the end() block of the chai's HTTP interface, we need to add the expectations for this API's response.

As with the add customer API's integration test, we can check the response status code to be successful with HTTP status code 200, and the data came out of the API call to be an array as we are trying to get the list of customers and it shouldn't be an empty list though. All the spec's expectations as described are written as shown below. Finally, to end this asynchronous HTTP call, we have to invoke the callback function done() at the of this test spec, within the end() block.

```
it('should get all customers', function (done) {
    request(app)
        .get(baseUri)
        .end(function (err, res) {

            expect(res.status).to.equal(200);
            expect(res.body).to.not.equal(unde-
fined);
            expect(res.body).to.be.a('array');

expect(res.body.length).to.not.equal(0);
```

```
        done();
    });
});
```

Eventually, we will have to see an error for the first failing expectation, status code 200, as we don't have any functional code in the controller for this API endpoint.

```
1) CustomerController
    GET /customers
        should get all customers:

    Uncaught AssertionError: expected 404 to equal 200
    + expected - actual

    -404
    +200
```

Code

To tackle the first failing test for the Get Customer List API endpoint, let's add the below code in the customer.controller.js file which will add a router definition for the GET HTTP method of the '/customers' endpoint, and also responds with the empty array once the call is completed.

```
router.get('/',
    function (req, res) {
        res.status(200).json([]);
    });
```

It will satisfy the few expectations of the test spec as we are getting an empty array response for the API call. However, still, we haven't completed the controller's router definition for getting the customers list from the express application. So we will see the next error as shown below when the test suites ran once again.

```
1) CustomerController
     GET /customers
        should get all customers:

   Uncaught AssertionError: expected 0 to not equal 0
   + expected - actual
```

To resolve the latest error, what we have to do is integrate the middleware method getCustomers() of the CustomerMiddleware in the router definition's handler methods. So insert the required middleware method just above the existing response handling middleware of the router definition of the '/customers' base URI, just like the completed code shown below.

Also, update the .json() method with the req.response object in the final middleware function as this object is assigned with fetched customers list from through model at the middleware function as you are already aware of.

```
router.get('/',
    CustomerMiddleware.getCustomers,
    function (req, res) {
        res.status(200).json(req.response);
    });
```

This code update will completely satisfy all the expectations of the newly written test suite for the get customer list API endpoint and yield all successfully running test scripts as shown below for the integration test cases for CustomerController.

```
  CustomerController
    POST /customers
POST /customers 201 29.041 ms - 228
      ✓   should add new customer (54ms)
    GET /customers
GET /customers 200 20.330 ms - 10306
      ✓   should get all customers
```

Step 06 - Get Customer List API - GitHub

YOU CAN FIND the code that we completed so far in the below Git-Hub repository. Please feel free to check out the whole codebase and explore this step's files in the **Step 06 - Get Customer List API** directory.

GitHub Repository:

https://github.com/parripandian/building-nodejs-api-with-tdd-approach

Current Step Directory:

https://github.com/parripandian/building-nodejs-api-with-tdd-approach/tree/master/Step%2006%20-%20Get%20Customer%20List%20API

Chapter 9: *Get Customer API*

9.1. Get Customer Functionality

WHEN WE CREATE the new customer in the API, we should be able to retrieve the existing customer details by somehow. This functionality is for that purpose. Unlike the Get Customer List functionality which doesn't need to pass the customer id as input, we need to know the unique identifier of the customer that was created with those details. We can note down this customer id from the response of when it was added. Also, using the 'Get Customer List API' endpoint to fetch all the existing customers in the system.

In this chapter, we will develop the code to get particular customer details by its id and the required unit and integration tests for all the layers involved in getting the customer details for the client request.

9.2. CustomerService - Fetch Customer By Id Unit Tests

IN THIS SECTION, we will start with writing test scripts and coding the required functional script for the CustomerService module file for Get Customer By Id functionality.

9.2.1. Unit Test 19: FetchCustomerById Success Test Case

We will start by adding test scripts for the customer.service.js file for the fetchCustomerById method.

Test Suite

Let's start with the test suite as usual. As mentioned in the sequence diagram of the service method for the Get Customer functionality, we can name the describe() block with the function name 'fetchCustomerById'.

```
describe('fetchCustomerById', function () {
    var expectedFetchedCustomer, customerId, ex-
pectedError;
});
```

There are a few variables required to be declared at the beginning of this test suite. These variables are for setting up the input like customerId and for the output for successfully fetched data and the error thrown for the failed execution path.

Test Script

Inside the main test suite's describe() block, we can start writing the test spec for testing the successful execution path of the service function fetchCustomerById(). Below is the completed test case script and we will go through each statement of it in the following section.

```
it('should successfully fetch the customer by id',
function () {
    expectedFetchedCustomer = CustomerFixture.cre-
atedCustomer;
    customerId = expectedFetchedCustomer._id;

    CustomerModelMock.expects('findById')
        .withArgs(customerId)
        .chain('exec')
        .resolves(expectedFetchedCustomer);

    return CustomerService.fetchCustomerById(cus-
tomerId)
        .then(function (data) {
            CustomerModelMock.verify();
            expect(data).to.deep.equal(expected-
FetchedCustomer);
        });
});
```

At first, we can populate the required variables with the test data fixtures. As we need the existing customer id to fetch its details from the database, we can use the createdCustomer test data of the Customer-

Fixture as it has the customer's unique identifier which is of the same format as the MongoDB's ObjectID for the customer document.

Once the createdCustomer data is assigned the to the expected-FetchedCustomer variable, which will also be used in setting up the behavior of the method under test as output response, we can get the '_id' attribute assigned to the customerId variable, which will have to be passed to the fetchCustomerById() method as input.

The next chain of method invocations is for defining the behavior of the mocked object CustomerModel. In this behavior definition, we are expecting that there will be a method 'fetchId()' with an argument for the customer id. And then, this formed query will have to be executed with exec() method before returning the document of the passed in customer id input.

Finally, we are calling the fetchByCustomerId() method of the CustomerService, and inside the handler function for the Promise's successful data return, we will have to confirm the mock object, CustomerModelMock's expected behavior by calling it's verify() method. Also, then we can compare the returned output data from the service method with the expectedFetchedCustomer.

So, we are supposed to get an error at this time for the latest test suite. Here is the screenshot of the error that we got.

```
1) CustomerService
     fetchCustomerById
       should successfully fetch the customer by id:
     TypeError: CustomerService.fetchCustomerById is not a function
      at Context.<anonymous> (tests/unit/customer/customer.service.spec.js:117:36)
```

Code

As a rule of thumb, when we see an error that something is not a function, we have to add the method to the module. Here, let's add the fetchCustomerById() method to the CustomerService.

```
module.exports = {
    createCustomer: createCustomer,
    fetchCustomers: fetchCustomers,
    fetchCustomerById: fetchCustomerById
};
```

Also, new function fetchCustomerId() will have to be added in the appropriate place after all the existing functions available in the customer.service.js file. As per the test spec, this method should be calling the findById() and exec() methods of the CustomerModel object in chained sequence and returning the promise.

```
function fetchCustomerById(customerId) {
    return CustomerModel.findById(customerId)
        .exec();
}
```

As shown in the above code block, the method under the test, fetch-CustomerById(), is satisfying all the expectation of the test suite that we have written in the previous section. It will make the new test run to pass all the test suites successfully. Below is the screenshot of the passing test suites of the CustomerService.

```
CustomerService
  createCustomer
    ✓  should successfully create new customer
    ✓  should throw error while creating customer
  fetchCustomers
    ✓  should successfully fetch all customers
    ✓  should throw error while fetching all customers
  fetchCustomerById
    ✓  should successfully fetch the customer by id
```

9.2.2. Unit Test 20: FetchCustomerById Failure Test Case

This section will cover the failure execution path of the fetchCustomerById() method. We have to test that how the method under test will behave when there is an error thrown from the dependency. It will make sure that the unit test covers both the negative edge case.

Test Script

To test the failure execution path, let's start with the test spec's it() block with an appropriate description of the nature of the test case. Inside this spec, we will assign the test fixture data of createdCustomer's '_id' to the local variable customerId which will be passed as the input parameter to the method that will be called in the test.

Also, we need to populate the error test data from the ErrorFixture to the expectedError variable which will be compared against the actual error thrown from the dependent method of the service method fetchCustomerById().

```
it('should throw error while fetching all cus-
tomers', function () {
```

```
    customerId =
CustomerFixture.createdCustomer._id;
    expectedError = ErrorFixture.unknownError;

    CustomerModelMock.expects('findById')
        .withArgs(customerId)
        .chain('exec')
        .rejects(expectedError);

    return CustomerService.fetchCustomerById(cus-
tomerId)
        .catch(function (error) {
            CustomerModelMock.verify();
            expect(error).to.deep.equal(expectedEr-
ror);
        });
});
```

Next step would be to set up the mock object's behavior except that this time it should reject it with an error thrown out of that method when its called. The behavior of the CustomerModelMock is configured in such a way that the two methods 'find()' and 'exec()' will be chained before it's rejection of the error object.

Finally, the CustomerService's fetchCustomerById() will be invoked with the parameter 'customerId', and the catch() block is used to capture the error with the handler function. Inside the handler function, the mock's pre-defined behavior is verified and the thrown error is checked against the test error data.

Code

Just like the previous unit tests for any service methods, this one also wouldn't need any specific functional coding for the failure execution path. It is because of the service method is just returning the dependency method call's promise as it is.

So, below will be the test result's screenshot after the current test suite ran successfully.

```
CustomerService
  createCustomer
    ✓  should successfully create new customer
    ✓  should throw error while creating customer
  fetchCustomers
    ✓  should successfully fetch all customers
    ✓  should throw error while fetching all customers
  fetchCustomerById
    ✓  should successfully fetch the customer by id
    ✓  should throw error while fetching all customers
```

9.3. CustomerMiddleware - Get Customer By Id Unit Tests

IN THIS SECTION, we will start with writing test scripts and coding the required functional script for the CustomerMiddleware module file for Get Customer By Id functionality.

9.3.1. Unit Test 21: GetCustomerById Success Test Case

The next unit test would be for the middleware function getCustomerById(). As per the modular approach that we have seen in the earlier chapter, middleware function will be dealing with the request and response objects to parse the inputs and set the output in the response object to be returned to the client.

Test Suite

Lets create a describe() block for the new test suite for the middleware function 'getCustomerById()'. We need to write the setup and teardown methods for the stubbed method of the dependency, CustomerService. Here are the completed initial scripts for the middleware function's test suite in the customer.middleware.spec.js file.

```
describe('getCustomerById', function () {
```

```
    var fetchCustomerById, fetchCustomerById-
Promise, expectedCustomer, expectedError;

    beforeEach(function () {
        fetchCustomerById = sinon.stub(CustomerSer-
vice, 'fetchCustomerById');
    });

    afterEach(function () {
        fetchCustomerById.restore();
    });
});
```

The declared variable fetchCustomerById is assigned with the stubbed method of the service inside the beforeEach() code block. Then the stubbed method is restored to the original method inside the teardown method afterEach().

Now, we are ready for adding the test suites for both successful and failure execution paths for the method under test, getCustomerById() of the CustomerMiddleware.

Test Script

Now, let's add a new test spec with it() block for testing the successful execution path of the getCustomerById() method. The below script should be inserted into the test suite that we just created in the previous section, below the afterEach() block.

In this test script, we assign the test fixture createdCustomer to the expectedCustomer variable which will be used for both setting the stub method's return object and also for comparing the returned data from the invoked method during the test execution.

```
it('should successfully fetch the customer by id',
function () {
```

```
    expectedCustomer = CustomerFixture.createdCus-
tomer;

    fetchCustomerByIdPromise = Promise.resolve(ex-
pectedCustomer);
                        fetchCustomerById.with-
Args(req.params.CustomerId).returns(fetchCustomer-
ByIdPromise);

    CustomerMiddleware.getCustomerById(req, res,
next);

    sinon.assert.callCount(fetchCustomerById, 1);

    return fetchCustomerByIdPromise.then(function
() {
        expect(req.response).to.be.a('object');
        expect(req.response).to.deep.equal(expect-
edCustomer);
        sinon.assert.callCount(next, 1);
    });

});
```

The next two lines are for programming the stubbed method fetch-CustomerById() of CustomerService which is a dependency of the current method being tested. As the service method will return a promise when it's called, we are setting up the stubbed method to behave like it's returning a promise and that promise will resolve to an output object, the test data expectedCustomer.

After the behavior of the stub is pre-programmed, the middleware function, getCustomerById() is called with the required inputs such as request, response and next. As this method should be invoking the service method to fetch the data from the customers collection, we are asserting this behavior that the service method is called once with the next line statement. It will ensure that the stubbed method is called once when the test it running.

Finally, we need to make sure that the method under test is returning a promise and its resolved output data will be handled with the then() block. Inside this handler block, we have to confirm that the returned data is an object as expected and it's equal to the test data expectedCustomer. So then, we are verifying that the next() callback function is invoked once at the end of the test.

Let's run the test suites now, and we will see the below error displayed in the test result.

```
1) CustomerMiddleware
    getCustomerById
       should successfully fetch the customer by id:
   TypeError: CustomerMiddleware.getCustomerById is not a function
     at Context.<anonymous> (tests/unit/customer/customer.middleware.spec.js:144:32)
```

Code

Let's start the functional code for the getCustomerById() by creating an empty function in the customer.middleware.js file and add it to the module.exports object just as shown below.

```
module.exports = {
    addCustomer: addCustomer,
    getCustomers: getCustomers,
    getCustomerById: getCustomerById
};

function getCustomerById(req, res, next) {
}
```

After adding these changes in the CustomerMiddleware module if we run the test cases, we should be getting the second error message as shown below for latest test suite as the code is not yet completed as per the test scripts are written.

```
1) CustomerMiddleware
    getCustomerById
      should successfully fetch the customer by id:
   AssertError: expected fetchCustomerById to be called once but was called 0 times
     at Object.fail (node_modules/sinon/lib/sinon/assert.js:96:21)
     at failAssertion (node_modules/sinon/lib/sinon/assert.js:55:16)
     at Object.assertCallCount [as callCount] (node_modules/sinon/lib/sinon/assert.js:137:13)
     at Context.<anonymous> (tests/unit/customer/customer.middleware.spec.js:146:26)
```

We

Let's continue adding more and required functional code in this file now. As the middleware function should be calling the service function to get the data from the database, we need to insert the fetchCustomerById() method invocation inside the newly created empty function getCustomerById().

Since the CustomerService's method will return a promise after fetching the data, we need to be writing the handler function for the successful path when the promise resolves to an output for this particular test case. Here is the completed code to resolve the latest error.

```
function getCustomerById(req, res, next) {

    CustomerService.fetchCustomerById(req.params.-
customerId)
        .then(success);

    function success(data) {
        req.response = data;
        next();
    }
```

}

As the current code satisfies the test spec's expectation, the new error should go away with all the test suites running successfully. Below is the screenshot of the latest test results for the CustomerMiddleware.

```
CustomerMiddleware
  addCustomer
    ✓  should successfully create new customer
    ✓  should throw error while creating the new customer
  getCustomers
    ✓  should successfully get all customers
    ✓  should throw error while getting all customers
  getCustomerById
    ✓  should successfully fetch the customer by id
```

9.3.2. Unit Test 22: GetCustomerById Failure Test Case

So far we have tested and coded the successful path of the getCustomerId() method for the CustomerMiddleware. Now, let's write the test script for the failure path of this method.

Test Script

We will have to start with it() block for the new spec with appropriate description. Below is the completed test script for the test case.

```
it('should throw error while getting customer by
id', function () {
    expectedError = ErrorFixture.unknownError;

    fetchCustomerByIdPromise = Promise.reject(ex-
```

```
pectedError);
    fetchCustomerById.withArgs(req.params.Cus-
tomerId).returns(fetchCustomerByIdPromise);

    CustomerMiddleware.getCustomerById(req, res,
next);

    sinon.assert.callCount(fetchCustomerById, 1);

    return fetchCustomerByIdPromise.catch(function
(error) {
        expect(error).to.be.a('object');
        expect(error).to.deep.equal(expectedError);
    });
});
```

Let's go over the above script in detail in this section. As we already know, we need to assign the expected output to the local variable. As this test is for the failed test case, we need to get the expectedError variable populated with the fixture test data for the error.

CustomerService's stubbed method fetchCustomerById is set up to be called with the input customerId, which is coming as a parameter from the client in the request and return a promise with rejected error out of it.

Then, the method under test is invoked in which the service method should be getting called once, and this is asserted at the next line in the test script. Finally, the error which is thrown from the dependent method with rejected promise call is handled by the catch() block. The thrown out error is compared with the expectedError inside the catch() block handler.

Running the mocha test suites will result in the below error as the functional code is not available to handle the rejected promise with the error object.

```
CustomerMiddleware
  addCustomer
    ✓ should successfully create new customer
    ✓ should throw error while creating the new customer
  getCustomers
    ✓ should successfully get all customers
    ✓ should throw error while getting all customers
  getCustomerById
    ✓ should successfully fetch the customer by id
    ✓ should throw error while getting customer by id
Unhandled rejection (<{"error":"Unknown","message":"Unknown ...>, no stack trace)
```

Code

As the new error shows that there is an unhandled rejection in the getCustomerById() method, if we add the catch() block with the handler function to the dependent service's fetchCustomerById() method call, we can resolve the error mentioned above.

Here is the completed functional code of the CustomerMiddleware's method which will satisfy all the expectation of its unit test.

```
function getCustomerById(req, res, next) {

    CustomerService.fetchCustomerById(req.params.-
customerId)
        .then(success)
        .catch(failure);

    function success(data) {
        req.response = data;
        next();
    }

    function failure(err) {
        next(err);
```

```
    }


}
```

Also, the final test result of the CustomerMiddleware module after the latest test case addition would be as below.

```
CustomerMiddleware
  addCustomer
    ✓  should successfully create new customer
    ✓  should throw error while creating the new customer
  getCustomers
    ✓  should successfully get all customers
    ✓  should throw error while getting all customers
  getCustomerById
    ✓  should successfully fetch the customer by id
    ✓  should throw error while getting customer by id
```

9.4. CustomerController - Get Customer API Integration Test

SO FAR WE have completed the unit test cases for all the layers in the backend service except the controller which is the API part of the RESTful service. So, to test the controller, we have to use the integration testing approach which means we cannot do any mocking or stubbing of any the dependent modules of the controller for the particular API endpoint.

9.4.1. Integration Test 3: Get Customer API

So far we have completed the unit test cases for all the layers in the backend service except the controller which is the API part of the RESTful service. So, to test the controller, we have to use the integration testing approach which means we cannot do any mocking or stubbing of any the dependent modules of the controller for the particular API endpoint.

Test Suite

For this functionality, to get a customer by its id, we need to call the HTTP method GET for an API endpoint. This end-point will have to have a parameter to map the customerId value. So that the same end-point URL can be called for different customers with their ids separately. The base URI for this endpoint would be '/customers/:customerId' where ':customerId' is the request parameter for a specific customer's id.

Below is the integration test suite for the GET /customers/:customerId API endpoint.

```
describe('GET ' + baseUri + '/:customerId', func-
tion () {

});
```

Test Script

To create the integration test spec for the current API, we need to start with it() code block with the baseURI for the Get Customer functionality as it's description. Here is the initial test spec for the API under test and it should be added inside the latest test suite's describe() block.

```
it('should get a customer by id', function (done) {

});
```

As this is a read-only functionality, means by calling this API endpoint there is no side-effect, so we need to use the GET HTTP method to call the URL along with the customerId.

To make the API call, we are using the chai's HTTP plugin's request object to create the request and response object to process the response once it's received. We have to form the URL with the baseUri and customerId as the path parameter to get the details of that customer.

Since this is an integration testing and we cannot stub/mock the response. When calling this API, it will go through the all the layers inside the REST service to get the document from the customers collection. To get a particular customer's information, we need to know the customer id of the customer. As we can't say that the primary and unique identifier of any customer affront all the time we run the test suites, we need to be somehow acquiring that id before this test suite runs.

There is one way we can achieve this dynamically without having to create a test fixture data for the customer id for this integration testing and also for the further API endpoints testing. If you notice the previous test suite that we have finished in the last functionality, Get Customers List, where we fetched all the available customers from the database.

What we can do in that test suite is, extract one of the customer from the fetched list and assign it to a global variable 'testData'. This variable with existing customer details in the database will have the customer id as well. This extracted customer's id can be used in this test case to fetch by the customer id.

As we discussed above, let's add the new variable testData at the top of the customer.controller.spec.js file just above the main describe() block. Let's declare this variable as an object with an object attribute 'existingCustomer'.

```
var testData = {
    existingCustomer: {}
};
```

Then, let's assign the first customer of the fetched customer list in the get customer list test suite and just above the done() call is made. Below is the statement that can be added.

```
testData.existingCustomer = res.body[0];
```

Now, come back to it() block of the current test case. Inside this block, let's add the completed test scripts as below. Here we are making the GET call to the '/customers/:customerId' where the ':customerId' named parameter is replaced with the customer id of the already fetched customer in the previous test case.

```
request(app)
    .get(baseUri + '/' +
testData.existingCustomer._id)
    .end(function (err, res) {

        expect(res.status).to.equal(200);
        expect(res.body).to.not.equal(undefined);
        expect(res.body).to.deep.equal(testData.ex-
istingCustomer);
        expect(res.body.firstName).to.equal(testDa-
ta.existingCustomer.firstName);

        done();

    });
```

After the asynchronous call to the API is completed, the expectations defined inside the end() block will get executed to confirm the behavior as defined for the controller's route definition for getting the customer by the id. The expectations are as usual: the response status code should be 200 for successful call completion, the response should be a non-empty object as we already know that particular customer exists in the system. Finally, the response body, which is the fetched customer details, should be same as the existingCustomer object of the testData.

Since we completed the integration test scripts for getting the customer by id functionality, we can run the test suites and expect it to fail for the newly added test case as the first expectation itself would not have been satisfied as we have not written any route definition for this API in the CustomerController yet.

Here is the screenshot of the first failure of this test suite.

```
1) CustomerController
     GET /customers/:customerId
       should get a customer by id:

   Uncaught AssertionError: expected 404 to equal 200
   + expected - actual

   -404
   +200
```

Code

So, now we need to write the functional code for the getting the customer detail by the customerId in the controller file. As described in the test spec for this functionality, the CustomerController will have to have a path definition fo the '/:customerId' with get method of the router() object.

This path will be handled by CustomerMiddleware's getCustomerById() method. Once the intended customer information is fetched via the CustomerService and CustomerModel layers from the MongoDB database's Customers collection, the retrieved data needs to set in the response object as JSON format along with the status 200 to indicate the operation is successful.

All these actions mentioned above are performed by the below code block which needs to be added to the customer.controller.js file after all the existing API endpoints definition, within the IIFE code block.

```
router.get('/:customerId',
    CustomerMiddleware.getCustomerById,
    function (req, res) {
        res.status(200).json(req.response);
    });
```

Since this code will satisfy all the expectations that we have added in the test spec for this API endpoint, all the failing test cases should be completed successfully now.

Below is the screenshot of all the integration test cases for the CustomerController including the latest test suite.

```
  CustomerController
    POST /customers
POST /customers 201 8.708 ms - 228
      ✓ should add new customer
    GET /customers
GET /customers 200 25.593 ms - 15802
      ✓ should get all customers
    GET /customers/:customerId
GET /customers/5b2b0b9d16373904dd090afa 200 7.728 ms - 228
      ✓ should get a customer by id
```

This test completes all the unit and integration testing needed for the Get Customer By ID functionality.

Step 07 - Get Customer By Id API - GitHub

YOU CAN FIND the code that we completed so far in the below Git-Hub repository. Please feel free to check out the whole codebase and explore this step's files in the **Step 07 - Get Customer By Id API** directory.

GitHub Repository:

https://github.com/parripandian/building-nodejs-api-with-tdd-approach

Current Step Directory:

https://github.com/parripandian/building-nodejs-api-with-tdd-approach/tree/master/Step%2007%20-%20Get%20Customer%20By%20Id%20API

Chapter 10: *Modify Customer API*

10.1. Modify Customer Functionality

IN THIS SECTION, we will start looking at the modify functionality of the Customer Service RESTful API. Once the customer document is added to the MongoDB collection, we should be able to alter its details as well. We will have to use the PUT HTTP method to do so when calling the API endpoint.

As this functionality will be coded in the modular structure, we need to write the unit test cases for all the layers from the controller to the service which will participate in modifying the customer information in the database. For all those components we will write the test specs individually to make sure everything is working as expected.

10.2. CustomerService - Update Customer Unit Tests

IN THIS SECTION, we will start with writing test scripts and coding the required functional script for the CustomerService module file for Modify Customer functionality.

10.2.1. Unit Test 23: UpdateCustomer Success Test Case

For this unit test, we will write the test scripts and functional code for the service method to modify the customer information successfully.

Test Suite

First, we will start with a new test suite for the CustomerService which will include the test specs for both the success and failure paths of the updateCustomer() method execution.

Below is the updateCustomer() method's test suite where we declared the local variables for the input, output and error objects which will be used by the two test specs for this service method.

```
describe('updateCustomer', function () {
    var existingCustomer, expectedModifiedCustomer,
expectedError;
```

```
});
```

Next logical step would be adding the appropriate test specs.

Test Script

As a first unit for the CustomerService, the successful execution of this functionality can be written as shown below. It () code block, with it's stated description says, contains the three-step process for a unit test.

At first, we defined the variables populated with the test data from the fixtures. The existingCustomer is for passing to the service method which will update the customer detail as input. To confirm the functionality of the method under the test, the second variable expectedModifiedCustomer is populated with the test data 'modifiedCustomer'.

```
it('should successfully update Customer', function
() {
    expectedModifiedCustomer = CustomerFixture.mod-
ifiedCustomer;
    existingCustomer = CustomerFixture.createdCus-
tomer;

    CustomerModelMock.expects('findByIdAndUpdate')
        .withArgs(existingCustomer._id, existing-
Customer, {new: true})
        .chain('exec')
        .resolves(expectedModifiedCustomer);

    return CustomerService.updateCustomer(existing-
Customer._id, existingCustomer)
        .then(function (data) {
            CustomerModelMock.verify();
            expect(data).to.deep.equal(expectedMod-
```

```
ifiedCustomer);
        });
});
```

Once the variables are set up, next, we need to set up the method with input parameter, expected behavior and the expected output object on the mocked CustomerModel object which will then be verified at the end of this test script execution.

As you might notice in it() block, after the variables definitions, the CustomerModelMock is expected to have a method 'findByIdAnd-Update' which accepts the customerId and the customer object which will be updated in the database and then it returns the updated customer information.

The mongoose Model has a method findByIdAndUpdate() which will query the document id which is passed as the first argument and update the object and returns the modified document because of the third argument '{new: true}'. If we don't pass this optional argument, the initially fetched document will be returned when this query got executed. We are mocking the behavior of this method with the chain of method invocations at this place inside the test spec.

Finally, we need to call the CustomerService's updateCustomer() method with the required input parameters. Inside this then() block which handles the successful response of the promise function, we are verifying the model's expected behavior and the confirming that the returned updated customer details are same as the expectedCustomer object. It concludes the unit test case script of this functionality.

Test Fixture

In the above script, we are using the test data from the modified-Customer of the CustomerFixture. If you notice, the content of this JSON file is empty as we have not added anything till this moment.

So, to make sure the test runs with proper test data, this file needs to be updated with appropriate customer information.

The below JSON content can be added to the 'tests/fixtures/customer/modified-customer.json' file to support this particular unit test.

```json
{
  "_id": "5a5ea8fde43c771e4aa5ea06",
  "firstName": "John",
  "lastName": "Smith",
  "email": "john.smith@example.com",
  "phoneNumber": 1234567890,
  "address": "401 W Street",
  "city": "New York",
  "state": "NY",
  "zipCode": "10000",
  "country": "USA",
  "__v": 0
}
```

As usual, this test case should fail if we run the Mocha test runner at this time with the error message as shown in the below screenshot for the CustomerService component.

```
1) CustomerService
     updateCustomer
        should successfully update Customer:
     TypeError: CustomerService.updateCustomer is not a function
      at Context.<anonymous> (tests/unit/customer/customer.service.spec.js:153:36)
```

Code

To develop the functionality for the updateCustomer() method in the customer.service.js file, let's start with creating the empty function with that name and add it to the module.exports object along with all the other methods available in this file.

Here is the empty function for updateCustomer() with the required input parameters as defined in the test spec. This method can be added at the end of the file after all the existing methods.

```
function updateCustomer(customerId, customer) {
}
```

Expose this method by adding this function name in the module.exports object so that this function will be visible to other modules., in this case, this will be used by the middleware method for updating the customer detail.

```
module.exports = {
    createCustomer: createCustomer,
    fetchCustomers: fetchCustomers,
    fetchCustomerById: fetchCustomerById,
    updateCustomer: updateCustomer
};
```

If we rerun the test, we would not see the previous error now as we have added the required code to resolve that error. Now, the next error message will be shown below because of the method under the test, updateCustomer(), is not yet completed with the expected behavior and the output.

```
1) CustomerService
    updateCustomer
      should successfully update Customer:
    TypeError: Cannot read property 'then' of undefined
      at Context.<anonymous> (tests/unit/customer/customer.service.spec.js:154:17)
```

So, this method needs to return a promise if you want the above message go away. As defined in the test script for this functionality of the service method, we need to invoke the dependent component CustomerModel's method. Here is the completed functional code which calls the model's method findByIdAndUpdate() by passing the customerId, modified customer information and the third parameter to return the updated document. Finally, the promise is returned after executing this update document query of the CustomerModel.

```
function updateCustomer(customerId, customer) {
    return CustomerModel
        .findByIdAndUpdate(customerId, customer,
{new: true})
        .exec();
}
```

This completed code will resolve the latest error message that we have seen before, and we will be able to see that all the expectations of the current test case are passed with the successful execution of the test scripts.

```
CustomerService
  createCustomer
    ✓  should successfully create new customer
    ✓  should throw error while creating customer
  fetchCustomers
    ✓  should successfully fetch all customers
    ✓  should throw error while fetching all customers
  fetchCustomerById
    ✓  should successfully fetch the customer by id
    ✓  should throw error while fetching all customers
  updateCustomer
    ✓  should successfully update Customer
```

10.2.2. Unit Test 24: UpdateCustomer Failure Test Case

Now that we have tested the successful path of the updateCustomer() method of the CustomerService module, we have to test the failure execution path as well.

Test Script

For the failure path test case, we need to write a new test spec with it() block with the appropriate description of this test. Inside this it() block we will have to assign the test fixture data to the variables that will be used in this test.

First, we will start with assigning JSON object to the variable expectedError from the unknownError test data of the ErrorFixture module. Next, we will populate the createdCustomer test data from the CustomerFixture module to the existingCustomer variable.

The next statement would be mocking the dependent method findByIdAndUpdate, defining the behavior with the required arguments and the expected output for the mocked CustomerModel object. In this mocked method the arguments are passed using the local variables that are created before. Also, there is another method exec chained in this mocked behavior with the output as the promise rejected with expectedError.

As the final step, we will have to invoke the updateCustomer() of the CustomerService module with the required parameters and capture the rejected error from the dependent method of the CustomerModelMock. Inside this catch block, we will be verifying the mocked model's behavior with the verify() method of its own. Also, we will compare the rejected error object with the expectedError variable to make sure that the method under the test is throwing the expected output.

With these statements, we can conclude the test scripts for the failure path of the service method. Below is to complete the test scripts for this unit test.

```
it('should throw error while updating Customer',
function () {
    expectedError = ErrorFixture.unknownError;
    existingCustomer = CustomerFixture.createdCus-
tomer;

    CustomerModelMock.expects('findByIdAndUpdate')
        .withArgs(existingCustomer._id, existing-
Customer, {new: true})
        .chain('exec')
        .rejects(expectedError);

    return CustomerService.updateCustomer(existing-
Customer._id, existingCustomer)
        .catch(function (error) {
            CustomerModelMock.verify();
            expect(error).to.deep.equal(expectedEr-
ror);
        });
});
```

Code

Eventually, we will not get an error as the functional code written in the last unit case will take care of this unit test as well. Because the updateMethod() is returning the same promise that was returned from the CustomerModel module and there is no other conditional execution path in this service method.

So, with all the test cases passed successfully, including this failure path unit test, below will the test result for the CustomerService module.

```
CustomerService
  createCustomer
    ✓   should successfully create new customer
    ✓   should throw error while creating customer
  fetchCustomers
    ✓   should successfully fetch all customers
    ✓   should throw error while fetching all customers
  fetchCustomerById
    ✓   should successfully fetch the customer by id
    ✓   should throw error while fetching all customers
  updateCustomer
    ✓   should successfully update Customer
    ✓   should throw error while updating Customer
```

10.3. CustomerMiddleware - Modify Customer Unit Tests

IN THIS SECTION, we will start with writing test scripts and coding the required functional script for the CustomerMiddleware module file for Modify Customer functionality.

10.3.1. Unit Test 25: ModifyCustomer Success Test Case

We will have to set up the test suite for the modifyCustomer() method of the CustomerMiddleware module first.

Test Suite

In this test suite, let's declare the local variables that will be used in the test scripts for this suite along with setup and tear down methods for the dependent method and inputs needed for the test cases.

```
describe('modifyCustomer', function () {
    var updateCustomer, updateCustomerPromise, ex-
pectedModifiedCustomer, expectedError;

    beforeEach(function () {
        updateCustomer = sinon.stub(CustomerSer-
vice, 'updateCustomer');
```

```
        req.body = CustomerFixture.modifiedCus-
tomer;
        req.params.customerId = req.body._id;
    });

    afterEach(function () {
        updateCustomer.restore();
    });
});
```

In the above test suite's describe() block, the variable updateCustomer is declared, and it's assigned with a stubbed method of the Customer-Service, which is the dependent module to perform the customer update operation. The input needed for the modifyCustomer() method of this middleware is assigned from the CustomerFixture's modified-Customer test data to the request's body object inside the beforeEach() block. Also, the same variable is restored inside the afterEach() block once each test case is executed.

Now, we are ready for the test specs for the modifyCustomer() method's both success and failure execution paths.

Test Script

In this section, we are going to write the test spec for the Cus-tomerMiddleware's modifyCustomer() method which will invoke the updateCustomer() of the CustomerService module to accomplish the task of updating the modified customer information in the Customers collection in the MongoDB through the CustomerModel object.

Let's create a new it() block for writing the test scripts for the current method under the test. We need to assign the values to the variables used in this test and set up the behavior of the dependent method that will be called to perform the update customer operation.

This setup includes the required input and output definition for that method.

Below is the completed script for this test spec where we begin by assigning the modifiedCustomer object from the CustomerFixture module to the expectedModifiedCustomer variable which will be used for defining the output behavior for the updateCustomer() method and also for comparing with output value once the same method is invoked by the modifyCustomer() method.

```
it('should successfully modify the customer de-
tails', function () {
    expectedModifiedCustomer = CustomerFixture.mod-
ifiedCustomer;

    updateCustomerPromise = Promise.resolve(expect-
edModifiedCustomer);
    updateCustomer.withArgs(req.params.customerId,
req.body).returns(updateCustomerPromise);

    CustomerMiddleware.modifyCustomer(req, res,
next);

    sinon.assert.callCount(updateCustomer, 1);

    return updateCustomerPromise.then(function () {
        expect(req.response).to.be.a('object');
        expect(req.response).to.deep.equal(expect-
edModifiedCustomer);
        sinon.assert.callCount(next, 1);
    });
});
```

As mentioned the above paragraph, we are defining the updateCus-tomerPromise variable as the successful response of the Promise resolved with the expectedModifiedCustomer variable. Also, this promise response is set to be returned as the output for the updateCustomer method of the dependent service module. Also, the inputs, the customerId and the modified customer object, are defined in the behavior of the stubbed method in the next lines of statements.

Inside this test spec, after the behavior definition, the method is called to test it out. Then, we are making sure that the middleware's method, modifyCustomer(), invoked the service method, updateCustomer(), only once when it's called.

At the last line of this test script, we have a handler method, then(), for the successful response of the promise when it got resolved with the output value. Inside this handler block, we are checking that the response attribute on the request object is an object with the exact copy of the expectedModifiedCustomer variable as per the defined the behavior of the stubbed method. Also, the number of calls to the next() function is confirmed to be precisely once.

With these different steps, the test spec for the modifyCustomer() method for the customer.middleware.js file is completed. The next step is to run the test scripts to make sure that there is an unsuccessful test result for the latest test case, which needs to be fixed in the next section.

Here is the screenshot of the current test result which shows an error for the latest test script added.

```
1) CustomerMiddleware
     modifyCustomer
       should successfully modify the customer details:
     TypeError: CustomerMiddleware.modifyCustomer is not a function
       at Context.<anonymous> (tests/unit/customer/customer.middleware.spec.js:194:32)
```

Code

In this section, we will develop the functional code for the modify-Customer() method by resolving the errors one by one. First, let's fix the 'TypeError: CustomerMiddleware.modifyCustomer is not a function' by adding a new empty function with that name after all the existing functions inside the customer.middleware.js file and expose the newly added function in the module.exports object of the Customer-Middleware module as shown below.

```
module.exports = {
    addCustomer: addCustomer,
    getCustomers: getCustomers,
    getCustomerById: getCustomerById,
    modifyCustomer: modifyCustomer
};
```

Here is the empty middleware function modifyCustomer() with the request, response objects and next function as input parameters as per the middleware function definition.

```
function modifyCustomer(req, res, next) {
}
```

Now, if you look at the test results, if the test runner keeps running or else start it again, you will notice that we don't see the above mentioned anymore and still, the test spec for the modifyCustomer() method will be failing, but, with a new error as shown below.

```
1) CustomerMiddleware
     modifyCustomer
       should successfully modify the customer details:
    AssertError: expected updateCustomer to be called once but was called 0 times
      at Object.fail (node_modules/sinon/lib/sinon/assert.js:96:21)
      at failAssertion (node_modules/sinon/lib/sinon/assert.js:55:16)
      at Object.assertCallCount [as callCount] (node_modules/sinon/lib/sinon/assert.js:137:13)
      at Context.<anonymous> (tests/unit/customer/customer.middleware.spec.js:196:26)
```

As per the above error which is based on the test spec's definition, the middleware method, modifyCustomer(), should be calling the service's updateCustomer() method once. So, let's add the statement to call the CustomerService's updateCustomer() method with parameters for customerId, which is coming in the request parameter and the modified customer object, which is coming in the request's baby object.

Since the service method returns a promise before it responds with the actual output, we need to add the handler function for the promise when it gets successfully resolved with the output. Below is the code required for this step.

```
function modifyCustomer(req, res, next) {
    CustomerService.updateCustomer(req.params.cus-
tomerId, req.body)
        .then(success);

    function success(data) {
        req.response = data;
        next();
    }
}
```

Inside the success handler function success() of the returned promise function, let's assign the output data returned from the service method to the response attribute in the request. This statement will satisfy one of the test script's expectation. For the last expectation, let's invoke the next() function at the end of the success() function.

With this code, we have satisfied all the expectations of the test spec for the modifyCustomer() method. So, if we start the test runner now, we should see all the test cases passed successfully and here is the screenshot of the CustomerMiddleware module's test suites' result.

```
CustomerMiddleware
  addCustomer
    ✓   should successfully create new customer
    ✓   should throw error while creating the new customer
  getCustomers
    ✓   should successfully get all customers
    ✓   should throw error while getting all customers
  getCustomerById
    ✓   should successfully fetch the customer by id
    ✓   should throw error while getting customer by id
  modifyCustomer
    ✓   should successfully modify the customer details
```

10.3.2. Unit Test 26: ModifyCustomer Failure Test Case

In the previous section, we have completed the successful execution path of the modifyCustomer() method. We need to test the failure execution path as well for the current method under the test.

Test Script

We will start with the new it() block for this test spec inside the modifyCustomer test suite for the customer.middleware.spec.js file. Below is completed the script for this test case.

```
it('should throw error while modifying customer by
id', function () {
    expectedError = ErrorFixture.unknownError;

    updateCustomerPromise = Promise.reject(expect-
edError);
    updateCustomer.withArgs(req.params.customerId,
req.body).returns(updateCustomerPromise);

    CustomerMiddleware.modifyCustomer(req, res,
next);

    sinon.assert.callCount(updateCustomer, 1);

    return updateCustomerPromise.catch(function
(error) {
        expect(error).to.be.a('object');
        expect(error).to.deep.equal(expectedError);
    });
});
```

As it's for testing the scenario for throwing the error by the dependent method call, let's fetch the unknownError test data from the ErrorFixture module and populate it to the expectedError variable.

Next two lines are set up the stubbed function's behavior. The dependent function updateCustomer() of the CustomerService is set to be returning a promise which will be throwing the error output when it gets rejected. At this place, the inputs are also set up by parsing the required data from the request's params and body objects.

Once the behavior setup is completed, the modifyCustomer() method is called with appropriate inputs for this middleware function. The number of times the updateCustomer() method called is asserted to be only once at the next line statement.

Once the function invocation is completed, the promise function returned by the dependent method call is handled with catch() block which handles the thrown error out of the updateCustomer() method call. Inside this error handler function, we are checking the rejected error is an object and is same as the expectedError variable.

With above two assertions for the expected behavior of the modifyCustomer() method, this test spec is completed. Also, below is the error message which you will see in the terminal as the test result for the CustomerMiddleware module.

```
CustomerMiddleware
  addCustomer
    ✓  should successfully create new customer
    ✓  should throw error while creating the new customer
  getCustomers
    ✓  should successfully get all customers
    ✓  should throw error while getting all customers
  getCustomerById
    ✓  should successfully fetch the customer by id
    ✓  should throw error while getting customer by id
  modifyCustomer
    ✓  should successfully modify the customer details
    ✓  should throw error while modifying customer by id
Unhandled rejection (<{"error":"Unknown","message":"Unknown ...>, no stack trace)
```

Let's fix this error in the next section where we will write the functional code to satisfy the expectations of this newly added test spec.

Code

To fix the error mentioned in the previous section for the modifyCustomer() method's failure execution path test case, we need to look at the same method in the customer.middleware.js file. As you might notice in the error message, the functionality code is missing the error handling code for any rejected error returned by the updateCustomer() call inside this function.

If we chain the catch() method along with the then() method for the service function call to handle the error thrown by the rejected promise, the latest error will be fixed. Below is complete functionality code for the modifyCustomer() middleware function with the required error handler correctly added.

```
function modifyCustomer(req, res, next) {
    CustomerService.updateCustomer(req.params.customerId, req.body)
        .then(success)
        .catch(error);

    function success(data) {
        req.response = data;
        next();
    }

    function error(err) {
        next(err);
    }
}
```

Now, since all the expectations of the new test case are resolved within the middleware module, the test result should show all the successfully passing test cases for the CustomerMiddleware module as shown the below screenshot.

```
CustomerMiddleware
  addCustomer
    ✓  should successfully create new customer
    ✓  should throw error while creating the new customer
  getCustomers
    ✓  should successfully get all customers
    ✓  should throw error while getting all customers
  getCustomerById
    ✓  should successfully fetch the customer by id
    ✓  should throw error while getting customer by id
  modifyCustomer
    ✓  should successfully modify the customer details
    ✓  should throw error while modifying customer by id
```

10.4. CustomerController - Modify Customer API Integration Test

IN THIS INTEGRATION test, we will test the modify customer API endpoint along with all the layers which help perform the customer update in the MongoDB database. Unlike the unit test cases for the individual layer components, we will not use any stubbing or mocking of any dependent module related functions, inputs or the outputs. When we run this test case, it affects the particulate customer document in the collection as if it's called from a client.

As we have mentioned in the low-level design for this functionality, we need to call this API endpoint with the HTTP PUT method for a customerId in the request parameter along with the changed customer details in the request body.

10.4.1. Integration Test 4: Modify Customer API

Let's start with the spec for testing the expected behavior of this API and then finally, adding the required code in the customer.controller.js file to meet the expectations of the test spec in the coming sections.

Test Suite

As usual, to add the integration test cases for an API in the customer.controller.spec.js file, we can create a new describe() block with

Parri Pandian

the description of this test case's purpose.

Add the HTTP method PUT with the baseUri of this express application and the customerId in the parameter for the description of this describe() block. It is the test that will be displayed while running the test cases and this will provide the clear indication of what each test suite that is getting executed.

```
describe('PUT ' + baseUri + '/:customerId', func-
tion () {
});
```

Inside this test suite block, we will be writing the integration test scripts for testing the Modify Customer API functionality.

Test Script

Now, we need to add the actual test script for the API end-point testing for the new test suite that we added to the /tests/integration/customer.controller.spec.js file.

A new test spec can be added with it() block as shown below. In this test case, the customer details update should be tested by calling the appropriate API end-point.

Before we start with the test script, let's prepare the input and expected output for this functionality, so that we can pass the required input parameters in the request and confirm the test result with the expected output object.

```
it('should modify existing customer', function
(done) {

    testData.modifiedCustomer._id = testData.exist-
ingCustomer._id;
```

```
request(app)
    .put(baseUri + '/' + testData.modifiedCus-
tomer._id)
        .send(testData.modifiedCustomer)
        .end(function (err, res) {

            expect(res.status).to.equal(200);
            expect(res.body).to.not.equal(unde-
fined);

expect(res.body.firstName).to.equal(testData.modi-
fiedCustomer.firstName);
            expect(res.body.address).to.equal(test-
Data.modifiedCustomer.address);

            done();
        });

});
```

If you know notice in the above-completed script, we are assigning the document's unique '_id' attribute to the testData's modifiedCustomer attribute from the existingCustomer attribute of the same testData object. Why do we need to do this step? You might ask. Since the customerId of the existing customer document is required so that it can be updated with the new information of the same customer, we need use the existing customer's id with the modifiedCustomer test data.

Here we are re-using the same testData.existingCustomer attribute that populated at the Get Customers List API endpoint's integration test suite before, which is in the same spec file. Also, the modifiedCustomer attribute should be added to the testData declaration at the start of this test file. Here is the updated testData object.

```
var testData = {
    existingCustomer: {},
    modifiedCustomer: CustomerFixture.modifiedCus-
tomer
};
```

Coming back to the test script, we are making the HTTP call to the modify customer API endpoint of the express application using the sinon's HTTP request plugin's put method. The URI for this call would be '/customers/:customerId'. Already fetched customer id is used as the parameter in this URI.

Also, the modifiedCustomer object of the testData is sent as the request body so that this changed details would be updated for the customer document identified with the customerId input.

As this is a synchronous call, we have to wait until the call completes. We can chain the end() block of this request utility to process the response once the HTTP call is completed. As usual, we need to confirm a few essential and necessary expectations of the response object of the called API end-point.

The first thing we need to confirm is the API call was successful, and it can be confirmed based on the HTTP status code 200. Then, the response body should be an object which is also should be same as the testData.modifiedCustomer attribute value. To be more confident that the customer detail has been updated successfully, we can check some of the customer's attributes against the expected modified customer details.

Finally, we have to invoke the done() callback function to inform the Mocha test runner that this particular test spec execution has been ended. With this call statement, we can conclude the spec scripts for this integration test case.

Here is the screenshot of the integration test case failure error as we yet to develop the required functional code in the customer.controller.js file for the modify customer API end-point.

```
1) CustomerController
     PUT /customers/:customerId
       should modify existing customer:

   Uncaught AssertionError: expected 404 to equal 200
   + expected - actual

   -404
   +200
```

Code

If you look at the error that we got for the current integration test, you would see the HTTP status code is 404 instead of 200. The error code 404 means that the API endpoint '/customers/:customerId' that we just called is not existing in the express application. So, let's fix this issue first and work through all the required functional code to satisfy the test spec's expectations one by one until we see the successful test run without any error shown.

As this is the integration test for the customer module, we need to add this endpoint router definition in the customer.controller.js file. In the CustomerController, let's add the new router definition for the '/customers/:customerId' path with the PUT HTTP method as below. Also, we need to add the response processing middleware to set the status code 200 along with the response from the request object.

Here is the first draft of the controller code to resolve the latest error.

```
router.put('/:customerId',
    function (req, res) {
        res.status(200).json(req.response);
```

```
});
```

When running the test suites, we will not see the status code 404 error again as we have added the required to handle that error now. Next, a new error will be shown for the remaining unsatisfied expectations that we have written in the test spec. Here is the screenshot of the new error for the CustomerController module.

```
1) CustomerController
     PUT /customers/:customerId
       should modify existing customer:
   Uncaught AssertionError: expected undefined to equal 'John'
```

By looking at the above error message, you would be able to figure out the missing functional code. The error says that one of the attributes of the output from the API call is not equivalent of the same attribute of the expected modified customer, which means, the customer detail is not yet updated in the database for the customer object passed as input in the request body.

As we already know that there is a middleware function available which will update the customer details as per the input information. So, let's make use of that CustomerMiddleware's method modifyCustomer() by adding to the stack of the handler functions for this API endpoint definition just before the last, output processing anonymous middleware as shown below.

```
router.put('/:customerId',
    CustomerMiddleware.modifyCustomer,
    function (req, res) {
        res.status(200).json(req.response);
    });
```

Now, if we run the Mocha test runner, we would see that there is no more error in the test result for the CustomerController module as the functional code written so far satisfies the whole test spec for the modify customer API endpoint. Here is the screenshot of the all successfully passing test specs for the controller of the customer module.

```
  CustomerController
    POST /customers
POST /customers 201 7.214 ms - 228
      ✓ should add new customer
    GET /customers
GET /customers 200 24.926 ms - 21756
      ✓ should get all customers
    GET /customers/:customerId
GET /customers/5b2b0b9d16373904dd090afa 200 3.018 ms - 228
      ✓ should get a customer by id
    PUT /customers/:customerId
PUT /customers/5b2b0b9d16373904dd090afa 200 3.151 ms - 228
      ✓ should modify existing customer
```

With this integration test, we have completed the test cases and functional code for the all the layers for the modify customer functionality. So far, we have tested all the components of this functionality individually with their unit test cases and also as a whole system with the integration test case.

Step 08 - Modify Customer API - GitHub

YOU CAN FIND the code that we completed so far in the below GitHub repository. Please feel free to check out the whole codebase and explore this step's files in the **Step 08 - Modify Customer API** directory.

GitHub Repository:

https://github.com/parripandian/building-nodejs-api-with-tdd-approach

Current Step Directory:

https://github.com/parripandian/building-nodejs-api-with-tdd-approach/tree/master/Step%2008%20-%20Modify%20Customer%20API

Chapter 11: *Remove Customer API*

11.1. Remove Customer Functionality

IT IS THE last functionality of the Customer Information Service. So far, we have developed the capability to add, get and modify customers to the database. Finally, we should be able to remove customer information from the backend as well. This section will be accomplishing that task.

To remove the customer from the MongoDB collection, we need to make use of the HTTP DELETE method. This method will indicate the API that the client wants to delete the customer document from the database which is identified by the customerId in the request path parameter.

Just like the all other functionalities, we will start with unit test cases and functional code for the components from the controller until the service layer. At last, we will complete this section with the integration test case for the API endpoint of this functionality.

11.2. CustomerService - Delete Customer Unit Tests

IN THIS SECTION, we will start with writing test scripts and coding the required functional script for the CustomerService module file for Remove Customer functionality.

11.2.1. Unit Test 27: DeleteCustomer Success Test Case

Let's start with the unit test script for the successful execution path of the functionally needed to remove the customer from the database at the service layer. So, we will prepare the new test suite for the delete-Customer() method in the customer.service.spec.js and then add the required test spec for this particular test case with appropriate expectations written within the test script to confirm the expected behavior of the method under the test.

Test Suite

As mentioned in the previous section, we need to start a new test suite for the service method inside the spec file. Below is the script of the test suite for the deleteCustomer() method which should be written inside the customer.service.spec.js file after all the existing test suites.

The new describe() block with the method name which is going to be tested will be written as below. We also have to declare the local variables needed for the test specs for both successful and failure execution path of this service method.

```
describe('deleteCustomer', function () {
    var existingCustomer, expectedError;
});
```

Test Script

Now, let's jump on to the new test spec for the deleteCustomer() test suite. This test script will be started with it() block with its intention added as the description as below.

First, the local variable existingCustomer is prepared with the test data createdCustomer json object from the CustomerFixture module. It will be used for both the input and expected output of the dependent method's mock.

As we will be utilizing the Mongoose Model's findByIdAnd-Remove() method to query the customer with its unique id and remove it once found, this behavior will have to be set up with the mocked object of the CustomerModel module. The next lines of statements are doing the setup as described above.

The fake method findByIdAndRemove() is pre-programmed at the CustomerModelMock object with the input of customerId from the local variable. Then the expectation of returning a promise is pre-programmed after the exec() method call is chained with the initial query method.

```
it('should successfully remove customer', function
() {
    existingCustomer = CustomerFixture.createdCus-
```

```
tomer;

    CustomerModelMock.expects('findByIdAndRemove')
        .withArgs(existingCustomer._id)
        .chain('exec')
        .resolves(existingCustomer);

    return CustomerService.deleteCustomer(existing-
Customer._id)
        .then(function (data) {
            CustomerModelMock.verify();
            expect(data).to.deep.equal(existingCus-
tomer);
        });
});
```

Finally, as the last lines of this spec, the CustomerService's deleteCustomer() method is called with the required input, and the expected behavior is confirmed with the verification method of the mocked object. Also, the expected output is checked to be equivalent of the exitingCustomer variable with the test data.

Running the test suites with Mocha Test Runner now will throw an error for this test case as shown in the screenshot below.

```
1) CustomerService
     deleteCustomer
       should successfully remove customer:
     TypeError: CustomerService.deleteCustomer is not a function
       at Context.<anonymous> (tests/unit/customer/customer.service.spec.js:189:36)
```

Code

To resolve the error shown in the previous section for the deleteCustomer() method of the CustomerService module, we need to add the new function in the customer.service.js file and expose it via the module.exports object. In this function, we can implement the functional code to satisfy the new test case's expectations.

Let's create an empty function for the deleteCustomer() inside the CustomerService module just below the existing methods. As we need the customerId to identity or query before deleting it from the MongoDB collection, we need to pass the customerId as an input to this function as shown below.

```
function deleteCustomer(customerId) {
}
```

Also, let's add this method to the module.exports object after all other methods. Here is the updated script for this module's exposed methods.

```
module.exports = {
    createCustomer: createCustomer,
    fetchCustomers: fetchCustomers,
    fetchCustomerById: fetchCustomerById,
    updateCustomer: updateCustomer,
    deleteCustomer: deleteCustomer
};
```

After these changes, we shouldn't see the same error message again when running the test cases. Instead, a new error message will be shown below. By looking at this error, we know its related to the promise function which is expected to be returned from the dependent method of the current function deleteCustomer() that's being tested and developed.

```
1) CustomerService
     deleteCustomer
       should successfully remove customer:
     TypeError: Cannot read property 'then' of undefined
     at Context.<anonymous> (tests/unit/customer/customer.service.spec.js:190:17)
```

As we have seen in the test case setup for the deleteCustomer()
method, this service function will make use of the CustomerModel's
findByIdAndRemove() method to query and remove the resulted
document of the query. This method will query the desired document
first, then remove it if found, finally return the found document.
Here, we need to need to pass the customerId to this mongoose
method as input, and also we need to chain another method exec() to
execute this query altogether to get the expected result.

Just by returning the same output from the model's method, we
could resolve the latest error as the CustomerModel's findByIdAnd-
Remove () method will return a promise as the response.

```
function deleteCustomer(customerId) {
    return CustomerModel
        .findByIdAndRemove(customerId)
        .exec();
}
```

Since we have coded all the required functionality of the deleteCus-
tomer() as per the test spec's expectation, there wouldn't be any more
error when the test suites are running once again. Below will be the
screenshot of the test results for the CustomerService module at this
moment.

```
CustomerService
  createCustomer
    ✓ should successfully create new customer
    ✓ should throw error while creating customer
  fetchCustomers
    ✓ should successfully fetch all customers
    ✓ should throw error while fetching all customers
  fetchCustomerById
    ✓ should successfully fetch the customer by id
    ✓ should throw error while fetching all customers
  updateCustomer
    ✓ should successfully update Customer
    ✓ should throw error while updating Customer
  deleteCustomer
    ✓ should successfully remove customer
```

11.2.2. Unit Test 28: DeleteCustomer Failure Test Case

For the unit test, we will write the test script for the failure execution path of the deleteCustomer() method of the CustomerService module. By doing this, we can ensure that our test suite for this functionality of the service module is covering all the execution path of the functional code.

So, any impact to this functionality by the changes made to this code in future will be captured during the development phase itself. It will force the developer to either fix the code which impacted the test scripts' expectation or update the test script for the changed functionality to meet the requirement specification as it evolves.

Test Script
Let's start this test spec with new it() block as below. In this test

script, we will have to assign the local variables with required test data from the respective Fixture modules. The variable expectedError is populated with the unknownError JSON data from the ErrorFixture module. The createdCustomer JSON data from the CustomerFixture module is populated to the existingCustomer which will be used as the input for the mocked function in the below statements.

```
it('should throw error while removing customer',
function () {
    expectedError = ErrorFixture.unknownError;
    existingCustomer = CustomerFixture.createdCus-
tomer;

    CustomerModelMock.expects('findByIdAndRemove')
        .withArgs(existingCustomer._id)
        .chain('exec')
        .rejects(expectedError);

    return CustomerService.deleteCustomer(existing-
Customer._id)
        .catch(function (error) {
            CustomerModelMock.verify();
            expect(error).to.deep.equal(expectedEr-
ror);
        });
});
```

In the next lines, the deponent method findByIdAndRemove() which needs to be called from the service method is mocked with expected behavior and expectations. The mocked method in the Customer-ModelMock is set up with the input of customerId from the expect-edCustomer variable and chained with the exec() method. Finally, it's expected to reject with the expectedError object.

In the last lines inside this test spec, we will write the script to invoke the CustomerService's deleteCustomer() method with the required input and then handle the rejected error with catch() block. The expectations of the CustomerModelMock is verified as per its defined behavior in the previous lines. Also, the thrown error from the mocked model's method is checked to be same as the expectedError object.

With these changes, we completed the script needed to test the expected behavior of the deleteCustomer() method of the service module.

Code

For the above test spec, if we run the test suites, we will not get any error. As there is no different execution path for its functionality as it just returns the same promise that its dependent method call returns.

So, here is the screenshot of the test results of the CustomerService module so far with all passing test cases.

```
CustomerService
  createCustomer
    ✓  should successfully create new customer
    ✓  should throw error while creating customer
  fetchCustomers
    ✓  should successfully fetch all customers
    ✓  should throw error while fetching all customers
  fetchCustomerById
    ✓  should successfully fetch the customer by id
    ✓  should throw error while fetching all customers
  updateCustomer
    ✓  should successfully update Customer
    ✓  should throw error while updating Customer
  deleteCustomer
    ✓  should successfully remove customer
    ✓  should throw error while removing customer
```

11.3. CustomerMiddleware - Remove Customer Unit Tests

IN THIS SECTION, we will start with writing test scripts and coding the required functional script for the CustomerMiddleware module file for Remove Customer functionality.

11.3.1. Unit Test 29: RemoveCustomer Success Test Case

As this is the first time we are going to write the test scripts for this new functionality in the customer.middleware.spec.js file, we have to start with the new test suite with initial testing scripts setup and tear-down code blocks.

Test Suite

Let's begin the test suite script with the describe() code block with required local variables, beforeEach() and afterEach () blocks with the code that needs to be executed before and after each of the test specs in this test suite.

As shown in the below initial set of scripts for this suite, we have few variables for the stubbed service method and its promise function along with the expected customer and error objects which will be used in each of the test cases for the middleware function.

```
describe('removeCustomer', function () {
    var deleteCustomer, deleteCustomerPromise, ex-
pectedCustomer, expectedError;

    beforeEach(function () {
        deleteCustomer = sinon.stub(CustomerSer-
vice, 'deleteCustomer');
    });

    afterEach(function () {
        deleteCustomer.restore();
    });
});
```

We created the stubbed function deleteCustomer() for the dependent service module using the Sinon's stub method. Also, inside the tear-down code block afterEach() we have restored the original deleteCustomer() method. This method will be called once each of the test spec execution completed.

Test Script

In this test case, we will be writing the script for testing the successful execution path for the middleware function of the remove customer functionality. As usual, let's start the test spec with a new it() block as shown below.

As the initial steps, we need to prepare the local variables with appropriate values. The variable expectedCustomer will be pre-populated with the test data from the CustomerFixture module. The next two lines are set up the expected behavior of the dependent method deleteCustomer() of the service module. As this service method is returning a promise after it deletes the customer from the MongoDB collection, the promise and the input and output behaviors are defined at these lines.

```
it('should successfully remove the customer', func-
tion () {
    expectedCustomer = CustomerFixture.createdCus-
tomer;

    deleteCustomerPromise = Promise.resolve(expect-
edCustomer);

deleteCustomer.withArgs(req.params.customerId).re-
turns(deleteCustomerPromise);

    CustomerMiddleware.removeCustomer(req, res,
next);

    sinon.assert.callCount(deleteCustomer, 1);

    return deleteCustomerPromise.then(function () {
        expect(req.response).to.be.a('object');
        expect(req.response).to.deep.equal(expect-
edCustomer);
        sinon.assert.callCount(next, 1);
    });
});
```

Then, the actual middleware method is called to test it out. After this method is invoked, we are verifying that the dependent middleware function, deleteCustomer() is called only once with the next line statement.

Finally, as the middleware function, which is being tested in this test spec, returns the promise we need to verify this output behavior with the then() function of the successful resolution of the promise. Inside this verification block, we are checking that the resolved output is an object and it's same as the expectedCustomer test data as defined earlier. Also, we are confirming that the next() function is called once after all the expected functionality is completed.

Now, let's re-run the test runner and see what the error is coming up for this new test spec is. As expected, we should see an error because of the latest test case added and below is the screenshot of the test results.

```
1) CustomerMiddleware
     removeCustomer
       should successfully remove the customer:
     TypeError: CustomerMiddleware.removeCustomer is not a function
      at Context.<anonymous> (tests/unit/customer/customer.middleware.spec.js:240:32)
```

Code

So, we got an error that there is no function exist with the name removeCustomer() in the CustomerMiddleware module. Let's fix this error by adding an empty method with the name removeCustomer and expose it to the module.exports object in the customer.middleware.js file as shown below.

```
module.exports = {
    addCustomer: addCustomer,
    getCustomers: getCustomers,
    getCustomerById: getCustomerById,
    modifyCustomer: modifyCustomer,
    removeCustomer: removeCustomer
};
```

Below is the empty removeCustomer() function added to the middleware module after all other existing methods.

```
function removeCustomer(req, res, next) {
```

}

When we rerun the test runner, we will not see the previous error, but a new one will be coming up as below. It's because we haven't added the required functional code as per the test spec's expectation.

```
1) CustomerMiddleware
     removeCustomer
       should successfully remove the customer:
   AssertError: expected deleteCustomer to be called once but was called 0 times
     at Object.fail (node_modules/sinon/lib/sinon/assert.js:96:21)
     at failAssertion (node_modules/sinon/lib/sinon/assert.js:55:16)
     at Object.assertCallCount [as callCount] (node_modules/sinon/lib/sinon/assert.js:137:13)
     at Context.<anonymous> (tests/unit/customer/customer.middleware.spec.js:242:26)
```

Based on the above error, we can understand that this middleware function needs to call the service method deleteCustomer(). Let's update the empty removeCustomer() method with the below content where the service method is invoked with the customerId parameter from the request object.

```
function removeCustomer(req, res, next) {

    CustomerService.deleteCustomer(req.params.cus-
tomerId)
        .then(success);

    function success(data) {
        req.response = data;
        next();
    }

}
```

Since we are testing and writing the functionality for the successful execution path, we will have to handle the successful resolution of the returned promise from the invoked service method. In this handler method success(), the output data is assigned to the response attribute of the request object so that this can be shared with the all the other middleware methods that are in the stack for this functionality. Finally, the next() function is called to pass the execution control to the following available middleware function.

Rerunning the test scripts will show that all the errors are fixed, and the latest test suite runs successfully as the expected behavior is coded in the middleware module for the remove customer functionality.

Here is the screenshot of the test results for the CustomerMiddleware module.

```
CustomerService
  createCustomer
    ✓  should successfully create new customer
    ✓  should throw error while creating customer
  fetchCustomers
    ✓  should successfully fetch all customers
    ✓  should throw error while fetching all customers
  fetchCustomerById
    ✓  should successfully fetch the customer by id
    ✓  should throw error while fetching all customers
  updateCustomer
    ✓  should successfully update Customer
    ✓  should throw error while updating Customer
  deleteCustomer
    ✓  should successfully remove customer
    ✓  should throw error while removing customer
```

11.3.2. Unit Test 30: RemoveCustomer Failure Test Case

264

So far we have tested the successful execution path of the removeCustomer() method of the CustomerMiddleware module. In this section, we will test the failure execution path of the same method which is under the test.

As we already have the test spec added for the removeCustomer() method in the customer.middleware.spec.js file, we will have to add a new test spec for this test case.

Test Script

Now we will add a new it() block for this test spec with appropriate description. Inside this test spec, let's pre-load the test data to the expectedError variable with the unknownError json data from the ErrorFixture module as this test is for checking the error handling path of the middleware function.

Next step would be to prepare the stubbed method's behavior with predefined input and output objects. As shown in the below-completed test scripts, we can set up the dependent method deleteCustomer() of the CustomerService module with customerId from the request parameter object as the input and the rejected promise object as the output. This promise will be returning the expectedError object as the rejected error when this service method is invoked within the middleware function under the test.

```
it('should throw error while removing customer',
function () {
    expectedError = ErrorFixture.unknownError;

    deleteCustomerPromise = Promise.reject(expect-
edError);

deleteCustomer.withArgs(req.params.customerId).re-
turns(deleteCustomerPromise);
```

```
    CustomerMiddleware.removeCustomer(req, res,
next);

    sinon.assert.callCount(deleteCustomer, 1);

    return deleteCustomerPromise.catch(function
(error) {
        expect(error).to.be.a('object');
        expect(error).to.deep.equal(expectedError);
    });
});
```

Once the input, output and the stubbed method's behavior is defined as described in the previous steps, we can call the CustomerMiddleware's removeCustomer() method with the appropriate inputs needed for the middleware function. Then, we need to assert the number of times the service method deleteCustomer() is called to be only once.

Since the method under test is called already, we need to check the returned promise object to confirm it's behavior whether it's same as defined earlier or not. Since the stubbed method is expected to yield a promise with rejected error object as output, we can compare the error object against the expectedError object inside the error handling catch() block of the promise object.

With these scripts, we are done with the testing script for the failure execution path of the removeCustomer() method for this functionality. Let's run the Mocha test runner and see the test results now.

Below is the screenshot of the test results for the CustomerMiddleware module after the latest test case has been added.

```
CustomerMiddleware
  addCustomer
    ✓  should successfully create new customer
    ✓  should throw error while creating the new customer
  getCustomers
    ✓  should successfully get all customers
    ✓  should throw error while getting all customers
  getCustomerById
    ✓  should successfully fetch the customer by id
    ✓  should throw error while getting customer by id
  modifyCustomer
    ✓  should successfully modify the customer details
    ✓  should throw error while modifying customer by id
  removeCustomer
    ✓  should successfully remove the customer
    ✓  should throw error while removing customer
Unhandled rejection (<{"error":"Unknown","message":"Unknown ...>, no stack trace)
```

Code

By looking at the error message in the lasted test result's screenshot, we can conclude that the rejected error is not handled as it's supposed to be. So, what we are missing in the removeCustomer() method in the customer.middleware.js file is catch() method call with the appropriate handler method.

As shown in the below completed functional code, we need to add the catch() method to handle the error and pass it to the error() function to handle it properly to avoid any such error as we have seen in the latest test run. As it's a middleware function, if any error occurred during the code execution, the error needs to be passed as the argument to the next(). So that the error will be handled by the app level error handling middleware function which was defined earlier in the apps.js file.

```
function removeCustomer(req, res, next) {

    CustomerService.deleteCustomer(req.params.cus-
tomerId)
```

```
        .then(success)
        .catch(error);

    function success(data) {
        req.response = data;
        next();
    }

    function error(err) {
        next(err);
    }

}
```

After the above code has been updated in the removeCustomer() method in the CustomerMiddleware module, running the Mock test runner will yield no more errors but all successfully passing test results for the middleware module of this express application as shown in the below screenshot.

```
CustomerService
  createCustomer
    ✓  should successfully create new customer
    ✓  should throw error while creating customer
  fetchCustomers
    ✓  should successfully fetch all customers
    ✓  should throw error while fetching all customers
  fetchCustomerById
    ✓  should successfully fetch the customer by id
    ✓  should throw error while fetching all customers
  updateCustomer
    ✓  should successfully update Customer
    ✓  should throw error while updating Customer
  deleteCustomer
    ✓  should successfully remove customer
    ✓  should throw error while removing customer
```

11.4. CustomerController - Remove Customer API Integration Test

WE ARE AT the last and final integration test case for the customer service API. In this test case, we will be writing the test scripts for the remove customer API endpoint without any stubbing and mocking of any of the dependent modules. So, when this test scripts run, it will remove the customer document from the MongoDB's customer collection. This way we can test the all the layers of the remove customer functionality with a single test script.

Along with the test scripts, we will also write the required functional code for the controller layer of this express application where the API endpoints are exposed for other clients' use.

As described in the low-level design for the remove customer functionality, we will be using the HTTP DELETE method to handle the API endpoint to delete the customer from the system.

11.4.1. Integration Test 5: Remove Customer API

Let's start with the spec for testing the expected behavior of this Remove Customer API and then finally, adding the required code in the customer.controller.js file to meet the expectations of the test spec in the coming sections.

Test Suite

We will start with a new describe() block to add the test scripts for the remove customer API endpoint of this RESTful service. As shown below, let's mention this test suite's nature in the description with the HTTP method DELETE and the API endpoint.

```
describe('DELETE ' + baseUri + '/:customerId',
function () {
});
```

After adding the above the test suite in the customer.controller.spec.js file, let's continue to the next section for completing the required integration test for the remove customer functionality of the customer service express application.

Test Script

Once we created the test suite as described above, we can add a new test spec for testing the remove customer API of the controller module. In this test case, we will compose the request with the chai's HTTP plugin with its delete HTTP method. Since the DELETE HTTP method doesn't require anybody content and only the API endpoint contains the customer id for the specific customer to be removed from the system.

Below test scripts show the completed spec for this integration test. Once the asynchronous call to the API endpoint is completed, we can define the expected behavior of the response object, which is returned from the API call, inside the end() block with an anonymous handler function.

```
it('should remove an existing customer', function
(done) {
    request(app)
```

```
        .delete(baseUri + '/' + testData.existing-
Customer._id)
        .end(function (err, res) {
            expect(res.status).to.equal(200);
            expect(res.body.firstName).to.not.e-
qual(undefined);

expect(res.body.firstName).to.equal(testData.exist-
ingCustomer.firstName);

            done();
        });
});
```

In this handler function, we have written the expectation statement for the API call's states code. As this test case is for the successful completion of the request, we can check that the status code is 200. Also, the remove customer functionality will have to respond with or without the body content as per the HTTP DELETE method; here we can expect the response body contains the customer document which has been removed by this API call.

This expectation will force us to implement the functional code to return the same customer object fetched from the database before it was removed. The next statement in the above test spec will check and confirm that the returned customer object is as per the test data expectedCustomer of this integration test.

Finally, let's finish this integration test by calling the done() callback of the Mocha test runner as this call will stop the test suite's execution.

Now, if we run the test scripts with the Mocha test runner, we will see the below-shown error message as a result of the new test case added in the customer.controller.spec.js file.

```
1) CustomerController
      DELETE /customers/:customerId
        should remove an existing customer:

   Uncaught AssertionError: expected 404 to equal 200
   + expected - actual


   -404
   +200
```

Code

Since we have got a 404 error in the test result for the new API end-point's integration test case, now, let's fix this error by adding the required functional code in the CustomerController module. As we are working on the remove customer functionality and the test spec is looking for the API endpoint with DELETE HTTP method, adding the below code will satisfy the initial expectation of the latest test case.

```
router.delete('/:customerId',
    function (req, res) {
        res.status(200).json(req.response);
    });
```

With the above functional code, we have added a new route definition with the delete method for the '/:customerId" in the customer.controller.js file after all other existing route definitions. We also have added an anonymous middleware function to process the final output and set it in the response object with the status code 200 to indicate this API endpoint's successful call.

Running the Mocha test runner now will show that that previous error is gone and few of the test spec's initial expectations are met as defined. However, still, we will see the below error for the remaining unmet expectations of the test spec.

```
1) CustomerController
     DELETE /customers/:customerId
       should remove an existing customer:
     Uncaught AssertionError: expected undefined to not equal undefined
```

Let's continue to add the appropriate functional code in the CustomerController module to fix the latest test error. If you have noticed
in the above code that we haven't called the middleware function to
remove the customer from the database yet. So, let's include the CustomerMiddleware's removeCustomer() method in the stack of middlewares in the current route definition just above the anonymous
and final middleware function.

Below is the completed code for the remove customer's functionality's route definition. This complete code will make the last error go
away as it satisfies all the remaining expectations of the test spec.

```
router.delete('/:customerId',
    CustomerMiddleware.removeCustomer,
    function (req, res) {
        res.status(200).json(req.response);
    });
```

Finally, running the Mocha test runner will show that all the test
suites are passed successfully as shown in the below screenshot. This
test result concludes the functional code for the remove customer
functionality's successful execution test spec.

```
  CustomerController
    POST /customers
POST /customers 201 4.462 ms - 228
      ✓  should add new customer
    GET /customers
GET /customers 200 18.984 ms - 27939
      ✓  should get all customers
    GET /customers/:customerId
GET /customers/5b3bdabfdfc01233c937b242 200 1.750 ms - 228
      ✓  should get a customer by id
    PUT /customers/:customerId
PUT /customers/5b3bdabfdfc01233c937b242 200 2.086 ms - 228
      ✓  should modify existing customer
    DELETE /customers/:customerId
DELETE /customers/5b3bdabfdfc01233c937b242 200 2.083 ms - 228
      ✓  should remove an existing customer
```

Step 09 - Remove Customer API - GitHub

YOU CAN FIND the code that we completed so far in the below Git-Hub repository. Please feel free to check out the whole codebase and explore this step's files in the **Step 09 - Remove Customer API** directory.

GitHub Repository:

https://github.com/parripandian/building-nodejs-api-with-tdd-approach

Current Step Directory:

https://github.com/parripandian/building-nodejs-api-with-tdd-approach/tree/master/Step%2009%20-%20Remove%20Customer%20API

Chapter 12: *Testing*

12.1. Testing

IN THIS SECTION, we will go over the testing related details. We will see how the test-driven development approach was used while developing the NodeJS RESTful service with MongoDB. Also, what is all the different testing methods are implemented along with the manual testing that yet to be covered in this section.

12.2. Unit Testing

SO FAR WE have written both the test scripts and the functional code for all the layers of the customer-service application. The unit test suites are implemented for all the layers except the controller. We also have completed test specs of execution paths for both the success and failure path to make sure that all the scenarios are tested to avoid any system failure.

These unit test scripts helped us develop the functional code for each of the methods to meet the expected behavior to accomplish their functionality. All the expectations of these unit test cases are carefully defined to align with the modular approach that we initially intended to achieve. The modular approach provided us with a guideline to well-define the role and the behavior of all the layer components to develop the modules in a loosely-coupled and yet cohesive manner.

Defining the behavior of each of the module in the unit test scripts provided us with the clear understanding of how the functional code needs to be written and what are all the input and output of the methods in each of those modules. With the test data fixtures, we have the flexibility to modify the test scripts very quickly and test any new functionality modification with minimal change.

Finally, we have written 30 unit test cases and implemented the functional code for all of them in the test-driven development approach as described in the earlier chapter.

Here are the unit test results for each of the components in the customer-service application.

12.2.1. MongoDB Module Unit Tests

Let's look at the MongoDBModule as this module was the first one that we started developing the test scripts and functional code. There are two test specs in this module: initial one is to test whether the mongodb.module.js file exists or not and the second one is to verify the MongoDBUtil module is available in this file or not.

This module file expected to expose all the components available in this module so that we can require only this mongodb.module.js file in any other component/module files to get the reference of any of its components.

```
MongoDBModule
  mongodb.module file
    ✓  should read the mongodb.module file
    ✓  should confirm MongoDBUtil exist
```

Using this single file in other files wherever it's required makes us develop less code and provide improved maintenance over the time as and when we add more components to that needed module. We can quickly get the reference to the new component file without adding it's relative path.

12.2.2. MongoDB Util Unit Tests

The next component file in the MongoDB module is the mongodb.util.js where we have the database initialization code, and it's invoked whenever the express application is starting up. As usual, the first unit test is verifying the presence of the mongodb.util.js file, and the next one is to confirm the init() function for the database connection initialization.

```
MongoDBUtil
  mongodb.util file
    ✓ should read the mongodb.util file
    ✓ should confirm init function exist
```

So, whenever we run the Mocha test runner, we will be able to confirm all the necessary files are in place to make the database connection during the application startup even before we run the application itself.

12.2.3. Customer Module Unit Tests

Now comes the unit tests of this RESTful service's main module, the CustomerModule. This module file contains six unit test cases right from the checking of the customer.module.js file's existence along with the expectation of the module file to expose an object which will contain the references to all the other components available in this customer module.

If you look at the below screenshot, we have individual files for all the components of the modular approach that we described in the initial chapter of this book. So, in this module file's test suite we have the required test specs for all the layers starting with the controller, middleware, service and finally the model components. All these test scripts will check and confirm these components' presence in this module before even we run any other unit test cases of each of the component files.

```
CustomerModule
  customer.module file
    ✓  should confirm CustomerModule function exist
    ✓  should confirm CustomerModule function returns an object
    ✓  should confirm CustomerController function exist
    ✓  should confirm CustomerMiddleware object exist
    ✓  should confirm CustomerService object exist
    ✓  should confirm CustomerModel function exist
```

As you notice in this customer.module.spec.js test file, we need to re-quire only this customer.module.js file to get hold of any of the components' reference in this module. This approach will avoid any clutter in the required section of the other module files wherever one or more of these components are needed.

12.2.4. Customer Service Unit Tests

Since mongoose will take care of the fetching and saving the document in the MongoDB collection without any other implementation for the CRUD operations of our own, as you already know during the development chapters', we only need to create the customer.model.js file with the required attributes or fields for the customer collection using the Mongoose's schema definition and model constructor. So we don't need to write any specific unit test scripts for the customer.model.js file

As the CustomerService module will use the CustomerModel to perform any CRUD operations on the customer collection, we have to develop the unit test cases for the customer.service.js file.

Below is the screenshot of the test suites result of the CustomerService. We have written ten unit test cases for all the methods available in this file. As per the requirements of this RESTful service described in the earlier chapter, we have five different functionalities developed in the whole API. To support all the required functionalities, the CustomerService module has five methods. So we have written two unit test specs per method for both success and failed execution paths for each method.

```
CustomerService
  createCustomer
    ✓  should successfully create new customer
    ✓  should throw error while creating customer
  fetchCustomers
    ✓  should successfully fetch all customers
    ✓  should throw error while fetching all customers
  fetchCustomerById
    ✓  should successfully fetch the customer by id
    ✓  should throw error while fetching all customers
  updateCustomer
    ✓  should successfully update Customer
    ✓  should throw error while updating Customer
  deleteCustomer
    ✓  should successfully remove customer
    ✓  should throw error while removing customer
```

All the test scripts results show that we have completed the required service component related methods for all the functionalities of the API functionalities and all are working as expected as well.

12.2.5. Customer Middleware Unit Tests

Now, let's look at the middleware unit test cases. In the customer.middleware.js file also we needed to develop the five required methods to handle the API functionalities.

Below is the screenshot of the CustomerMiddleware component's unit test results shows that we have accomplished the task mentioned above as well. With two test cases per method for both success and failure execution paths, we have completed ten test cases for all five methods of the middleware layer of the Customer Information Service.

```
CustomerMiddleware
  addCustomer
    ✓  should successfully create new customer
    ✓  should throw error while creating the new customer
  getCustomers
    ✓  should successfully get all customers
    ✓  should throw error while getting all customers
  getCustomerById
    ✓  should successfully fetch the customer by id
    ✓  should throw error while getting customer by id
  modifyCustomer
    ✓  should successfully modify the customer details
    ✓  should throw error while modifying customer details
  removeCustomer
    ✓  should successfully remove the customer
    ✓  should throw error while removing customer
```

There is only one layer above the middleware available in this express application, which is the controller layer according to our modular approach. This layer of the component cannot be tested with the mocking or stubbing of dependency modules, we have added the controller component's test cases into the integration test. So the unit testing scope is stopping at the middleware layer's component. We can go over these integration test case details in the next section.

12.3. Integration Testing

SO FAR WE have gone through all the unit test cases for the service and middleware components of the system. We haven't added any unit test scripts for the controller component because of the nature of the CustomerController module. Since we cannot mock or stub the behavior of middleware methods that are added to the stack of the route definitions what we can test at this layer is the integration testing.

As you know, unlike the unit test scripts, when we run the integration test it will test the all the layers of the particular functionality as a whole. The controller component consists of the route definitions for each of the functionality it offers as API endpoints, which can be called by any of the external clients. So we need to make the HTTP request to these API endpoints to perform the integration testing with appropriate inputs and expected outputs.

12.3.1. Customer Controller Integration Tests

In this section, we will look into the integration test scripts for the controller component of the customer information service. As you see in the below screenshot of the CustomerController's test results, we have successfully tested all the endpoints of the RESTful service's API.

In these integration test scripts, we have used the Sinon's request and response plugins to prepare the HTTP requests for the API endpoints and process the response object returned from the asynchronous calls.

```
CustomerController
    POST /customers
POST /customers 201 7.694 ms - 228
    ✓   should add new customer
    GET /customers
GET /customers 200 48.473 ms - 27939
    ✓   should get all customers (53ms)
    GET /customers/:customerId
GET /customers/5b5bd065e556821851954d8d 200 3.204 ms - 228
    ✓   should get a customer by id
    PUT /customers/:customerId
PUT /customers/5b5bd065e556821851954d8d 200 5.029 ms - 228
    ✓   should modify existing customer
    DELETE /customers/:customerId
DELETE /customers/5b5bd065e556821851954d8d 200 4.484 ms - 228
    ✓   should remove an existing customer
```

As you can see from the above screenshot, we have used the appropriate HTTP methods for each of the functionalities of the API as defined in the RESTful service's chapter. All the CRUD operations of the API are implemented as per the REST principles as described below.

1. Created a new customer with POST HTTP method

2. Retrieved the existing customers with GET HTTP method

3. Updated an existing customer with PUT HTTP method

4. Deleted an existing customer with the DELETE HTTP method

So, we have completed the five integration test scripts with functional code implementation for the all the functionalities of the customer information system as discussed in the requirements chapter.

12.3.2. Integration Testing With Mock Database

So far we have gone through unit test cases for the all the layers below the controller and integration test cases for the controller layer which provides the API endpoints of the customer information RESTful service.

If you look into the MongoDB's customer collection, you will find that each time integration test suites run the documents are being created, modified, fetched or deleted based on the individual test suite. It means that we are testing the express application with the real database integration by not only testing all the modules for each of the API endpoints but also testing the database operation for all the functionalities that API provides.

If we keep running the test suites for all the changes, we might keep accumulating the documents in the database. Also, it may not be advisable to spin-up a dedicated database for running the integration test only. So, what can we do to handle this situation?

There is an option available for this situation. We can use an in-memory MongoDB database for running the integration test suites. In this way, we can test the system as a whole without persisting any documents in the database. Also, we can get the clean in-memory database up and running each time we run the integration test suites. This capability provides us for initializing the database state specific to each and every test suite that we run, if we need.

So, how do we set up the in-memory MongoDB database for our customer information service's integration test suites? Lets' follow the below instructions.

First, tests/integration/customer.controller.spec.js file, we need to add the below require statements along with defining few local variables. We need two new modules: mongoose and mockgoose-fix as these modules will be helping us to initialize the connection to the in-memory MongoDB instance.

```
var Mongoose = require('mongoose').Mongoose;
var Mockgoose = require('mockgoose-fix').Mockgoose;
var mongoose = new Mongoose;
var mockgoose = new Mockgoose(mongoose);
```

As we already have installed the mongoose module, let's install the mockgoose-fix module for testing purpose only by running the below command in the terminal from the root path of our express application. This module provides the in-memory database when MongoDBUtil module executes the mongoose.connect() statement to initialize the MongoDB database connection. So we can run the integration tests without connecting to the real database.

```
npm install mockgoose-fix --save-dev
```

Once the required modules and variables made available to the customer.controller.spec.js file, let's configure the needed attributes for the mongoose and mockgoose modules as below. With the first line, we are loading the promise module to the mongoose from the global module available to the NodeJS environment. Also, we are setting the mongo database version as 3.4.3 as this version is working successfully for mocking the test database at the time of writing this book.

```
mongoose.Promise = global.Promise;
mockgoose.helper.setDbVersion('3.4.3');
```

Finally, with below code block, we can complete the in-memory test database for our integration testing. To create the in-memory database, we still need to have the running MongoDB server's URL, but there is no need to have any database instance available in that server. So the database name mockDatabaseDB mentioned in the below mockMongoDBURL variable does need to be existing in the database server localhost:32768.

```
var mockMongoDBURL = 'mongodb://localhost:32768/
mockCustomerDB';

before(function (done) {
    mockgoose.prepareStorage().then(function () {
        mongoose.connect(mockMongoDBURL, {}, func-
tion (err) {
            done(err);
        });
    })
});
```

In the before() code block above, mockgoose will prepare the in-memory test database instance when mockgoose intercepts the mongoose.-connect() statement gets executed. This code block will take care of the MongoDB database connection when any of the integration test suites runs.

As the in-memory database instance will be running whenever the integration test suites in the customer.controller.spec.js file run, the CRUD operations for all the API endpoint functionalities will be performed in the test databased itself without any integration to the real database. This capability provides the clean database for all the integration test specs all the time the test suites run.

Step 10 - Integration Testing With Database - GitHub

YOU CAN FIND the code that we completed so far in the below GitHub repository. Please feel free to check out the whole codebase and explore this step's files in the **Step 10 - Integration Testing With Mock Database** directory.

GitHub Repository:

https://github.com/parripandian/building-nodejs-api-with-tdd-approach

Current Step Directory:

https://github.com/parripandian/building-nodejs-api-with-tdd-approach/tree/master/Step%2010%20-%20Integration%20Testing%20With%20Mock%20Database

12.4. API Testing

SO FAR WE have been testing at the unit and integration level for the Customer Information Service. All these testings are done without even starting the express application. With the unit testing, we checked and confirmed that all the individual components are working as expected for each of the functionalities.

Also, with integration testing, we tested the API endpoints which expose the functionalities as a whole system. The integration testing also confirms that all the individual layers of components are working together to accomplish the expected functionality for each of the API endpoints.

Are these testing enough to conclude that the RESTful service is working as designed? Of course, yes. Since the integration testing is performed from the client perspective to validate the implemented behavior is working as expected, we can decide to stop the testing effort at this level.

Although all the necessary testing has been performed for the customer information service, it wouldn't hurt to run another set of testing for this service. The new set of testing would be API testing.

In the API testing, we would be testing the API endpoints outside the development environment by running the RESTful service. It can be a manual testing or automated testing by making the HTTP calls to all the API endpoints that this service provides to the client. So, this testing is done to validate the API from the client perspective by running the test suites outside the development environment. We will go through the API testing with the third-party utility called Postman.

12.4.1. API Testing With Postman

There are several API development environment tools available for developers to design, mock, debug, test, publish, monitor and document the APIs with the API-first approach. Postman is one of such tools available for API developers which can be downloaded from the https://www.getpostman.com/ website. We will be using this tool to test our customer information service API.

Before we test our API, we need to run the RESTful service's server by running the below command in the terminal under the root path of the customer service express application.

```
npm start
```

Once the server is up and running, check the service with the http://localhost:3000/ link and verify that you see the below content in the browser.

```
{
    "name": "customer-service",
    "version": "0.0.0",
    "status": "up"
}
```

Customer Service Collection

As a first step for the API testing with the postman, let's create a new collection called 'customer-service' so that all the requests for the available API endpoints can be added to this collection.

You can refer this link https://www.getpostman.com/docs/v6/ postman/collections/creating_collections to know more detailed steps about creating a new collection in the postman application. At the end of this tutorial as mentioned in the above link, you would have created a new collection as shown in the below screenshot.

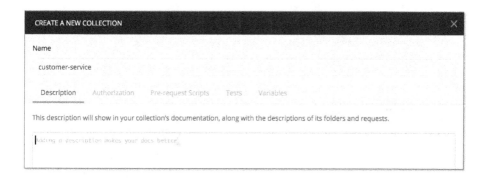

12.4.2. Add Customer API Testing

The first API endpoint we will be testing with the Postman is Add Customer API. What we need to start the testing is that URL for adding the customer and the JSON content of the customer information to pass to the endpoint.

As shown in the below screenshot, let's create a new request for the Add Customer endpoint. Below are the steps to do so.

1. Add a new tab by clicking the '+' sign on the top of the page.
2. Select the **POST** method from the drop-down.
3. Enter the Add Customer endpoint URL of the running customer service express application. In this case, the URL is **http://localhost:3000/customers**
4. Copy the content of the **tests/fixtures/customer/new-cus-**

tomer.json file and paste it in the body as raw content and make sure the content type is selected as **JSON(application/ json)**. You can change any of the copied JSON attributes in the body section if you want.

5.   Then click the **Save** button. In the popup, enter the request name and description, and then select the customer-service to add this request to it. Also, finally, click the Save button in the popup.

6.   Click the **Send** button to send this POST request with the new customer information in the body as JSON object to the customer-service application. Once the customer is added to the system, the response will be shown with the newly added customer details in the response body section.

As there are multiple ways to create a new request in the Postman, please refer this link https://www.getpostman.com/docs/v6/postman/sending_api_requests/requests on how to send the API requests.

With these steps implemented, we have completed the first API testing with the Postman application. We will follow the same set of steps for the remaining API endpoints as well.

12.4.3. Get Customer List API Testing

The next API endpoint we will be testing with the Postman is Get Customer List API. As this endpoint is associated with the GET HTTP method, there is no content in the body needed when sending a request to this endpoint.

As shown in the below screenshot, let's create a new request for the Get Customer List endpoint. Follow these steps to do so.

1. Add a new tab by clicking the '+' sign on the top of the page.
2. Select the **GET** method from the drop-down.
3. Enter the Get Customer List endpoint URL of the running customer service express application. In this case, the URL is **http://localhost:3000/customers,** same as the Add Customer URL.
4. Then click the **Save** button. In the popup, enter the request name as 'Get Customer List' and any description, then select the customer-service to add this request to it. Also, finally, click the Save button in the popup.
5. Click the **Send** button to send this GET request to get the list of customers from the customer-service application. Once the request is completed, the response will be shown with the list of customers in the response body section.

1.

This testing concludes the Get Customer List API testing with the Postman application.

12.4.4. Get Customer API Testing

In the last section, we fetched all the customers from the Customer Information System. Now, let's look at the testing of the API endpoint which will retrieve a customer with the customer's identifier. As this endpoint is also associated with the GET HTTP method, there is no content in the body needed when sending a request to this endpoint, but we need to send the customer's id in the path parameter.

As shown in the below screenshot, let's create a new request for the Get Customer By Id endpoint. Follow these steps to do so.

1.   Add a new tab by clicking the '+' sign on the top of the page.
2.   Select the **GET** method from the drop-down.
3.   Enter the Get Customer By Id endpoint URL of the running customer service express application. In this case, the URL is

http://localhost:3000/customers/{customerId}. Here the {customerId} can be any of the customer id from the previous testing.

4. Then click the **Save** button. In the popup, enter the request name as 'Get Customer By Id' and any description, then select the customer-service to add this request to it. Finally, click the Save button in the popup.

5. Click the **Send** button to send this GET request to get the particular customer information from the customer-service application using the customer id. Once the request is completed, the response will be shown with the found customer details in the response body section.

We have completed the Get Customer By Id API testing in the Postman application.

12.4.5. Modify Customer API Testing

So far we have tested the Add Customer and Get Customer By Id API endpoints. For this API testing, the above two tests are a prerequisite because this new API testing is about updating the existing customer's details. In this testing, we will be updating the customer that we created with the Add Customer testing and with the same URL as the Get Customer By Id API testing with PUT HTTP method.

As shown in the below screenshot, let's create a new request for the Modify Customer endpoint. Below are the steps to accomplish this testing task.

1. Add a new tab by clicking the '+' sign on the top of the page.
2. Select the **PUT** method from the drop-down.
3. Enter the Modify Customer endpoint URL of the running customer service express application. In this case, the URL is **http://localhost:3000/customers/{customerId}**. Here the {customerId} can be any of the customer id from the previous testing same as the Get Customer By Id API Testing.
4. Copy the response body content from the previous Get Customer By Id API testing and paste it into this request's body section. You can change any of the JSON attributes of the customer details to test the modify API endpoint.
5. Then click the **Save** button. In the popup, enter the request name as 'Modify Customer' and any description, then select the customer-service to add this request to it. Finally, click the Save button in the popup.
6. Click the **Send** button to send this PUT request to update the particular customer information to the customer-service application using the customer id and modified details in the request body. Once the request is completed, the response will be shown with the changed customer details in the response body section.

Now, the Modify Customer API is completed successfully with the Postman application.

12.4.6. Remove Customer API Testing

Let's go over the last and final API testing with Postman by removing the existing customer from the system by sending the request to the API endpoint associated with the DELETE HTTP method. For this testing also, we will be using the same URL as the Modify Customer API testing except for the request body content as the DELETE HTTP method doesn't accept anybody content in the request.

As shown in the below screenshot, let's create a new request for the Modify Customer endpoint. Below are the steps to accomplish this testing task.

1. Add a new tab by clicking the '+' sign on the top of the page.
2. Select the **DELETE** method from the drop-down.
3. Enter the Remove Customer endpoint URL of the running cus-

tomer service express application. In this case, the URL is **http://localhost:3000/customers/{customerId}**. Here the {cus-tomerId} can be same customer id of the previous Modify Customer API testing.

4. Then click the **Save** button. In the popup, enter the request name as 'Remove Customer' and any description, then select the customer-service to add this request to it. Finally, click the Save button in the popup.

5. Click the **Send** button to send this DELETE request to remove the particular customer information from the customer-service application using the customer id. Once the request is completed, the response will be shown with the deleted customer details in the response body section.

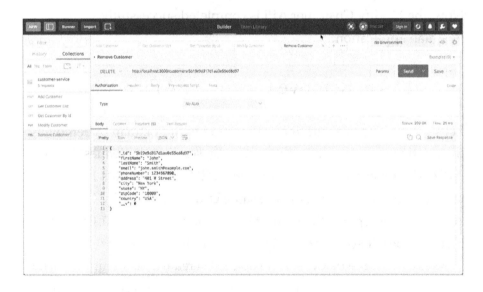

Finally, with this API testing, we conclude all the API testing in the Postman for all the API endpoints of the Customer Information System.

Chapter 13: *Conclusion*

13.1. Conclusion

HOW WAS THE experience of building the Node.js REST API with TDD approach?

Did I keep my assurance of providing you with the enjoyable learning experience throughout this book?

Finally and most importantly, did you enjoy your journey of this book?

I hope, this book met your initial expectation when you bought it. Also, I assume that you have learned how to build the Node.js RESTful API with Test-Driven Development approach and you will be using the concepts and process that you learned in this book to advance your career.

Appreciate your time and effort that you spent in this book.